# Rising

# Ris

## From a Mud Hut to the Boardroom— and Back Again

*A Memoir*

# ing

## GRACI HARKEMA

● ● PAGE TWO

Some names and identifying details have been
changed to protect the privacy of individuals.

Cataloguing in publication information is
available from Library and Archives Canada.
ISBN 978-1-77458-251-0 (hardcover)
ISBN 978-1-77458-252-7 (ebook)
ISBN 978-1-77458-275-6 (audiobook)

Page Two
pagetwo.com

Edited by Emily Schultz
Copyedited by Melissa Kawaguchi
Proofread by Alison Strobel
Jacket and interior design by Jennifer Lum
Jacket photos by Brian Kelly
All interior photos courtesy of Graci Harkema, unless otherwise credited
Printed and bound in Canada by Friesens
Distributed in Canada by Raincoast Books
Distributed in the US and internationally by Macmillan

23 24 25 26 27   5 4 3 2 1

graciharkema.com

*To anyone who has been overlooked,*
*marginalized, and underrepresented.*
*I wrote this book for you.*

*In my darkest of hours, I thought I was alone.*
*If you have been through trauma and turmoil,*
*know that even when it feels like you are in a cyclone*
*of solitude, you are not alone.*

*I see you. I value you. I am with you.*

# Contents

# 1

# Divine Timing

"Only when we are brave enough to explore the darkness will we discover the infinite power of our light."

**BRENÉ BROWN**

THE RED-COLORED EARTH patched with sticks, straw, and grass created the ten-foot diameter of the circular mud hut where I took my first breath as I entered this world in the Democratic Republic of the Congo, then called Zaire. I was born on July 3, 1985, in central Africa near the border of the Congo and Rwanda, about a decade prior to the peak of the horrific Rwandan Genocide, where a million men, women, and children were killed based on their tribal identity, during the span of three months. The area I was born in was a place where violence, riots, war, rebellion, refugees, sex trafficking, abuse, and extreme poverty ran rampant.

My biological mother, MariJani, was extremely impoverished, living in the mud hut, and didn't have anything except for prayers for her next breath. She had grieved the loss of many family members who died from disease and malnutrition. MariJani was not involved with my biological father; in fact, he was unknown to her. She was young when she unexpectedly got pregnant with me. It is common in Bukavu for men to overpower young women. Women and young girls are treated as second-class citizens, and they are expected to carry children and serve men's needs, no matter what.

My less-than-four-pounds, frail body was prematurely delivered in the darkness of the mud hut from MariJani's weak, thin, malnourished frame. From the moment I took my first breath, MariJani was also fighting for hers. She was stricken with a fatal protein deficiency disease. Both MariJani and I had a slim chance of survival.

I was fighting oral thrush, which was inhibiting me from being able to suck, swallow, and digest anything for the first several weeks of my life. My body would later learn to fight more illnesses, including malaria and hepatitis. MariJani's dire condition made it impossible for her to care for me—at one week old, the only chance I had at survival was from the torturous and selfless decision she made to hand me over to her mother to find care for me. Desperate for help, my biological grandmother went from neighbor to neighbor across the village seeking aid and support to make sure I lived. A neighbor heard of an orphanage down the mountain, and the folks there could potentially even give my biological grandmother food, since she was also weak from malnutrition.

My biological grandmother walked several hours through the bush and through the mountainous terrain above Lake Kivu. There I was, one week old, frail, and nameless; there she was, hoping I would survive as she brought me to an orphanage in the village of Kidodobo, in the Walungu territory, for a chance of care.

Illness was very prevalent in newborns. No newborn had survived the cold of the high elevation, and most died within twenty-four hours. When we arrived at the orphanage, the concerned, caring orphanage workers did not want me near the other children as they were fearful I could catch something from them and die. They placed me in their home next door to

There I was, one week
old, frail, and nameless;
there she was, hoping I would
survive as she brought me
to an orphanage.

the orphanage in a bedroom near the bathroom, in a toy baby doll bassinet that belonged to one of daughters of the missionary couple who ran the orphanage.

A couple of hours after I arrived at the orphanage, an American couple named Ray and Jayn Harkema with their four children, ages seven to fifteen, traveled a few hours from their home in Bukavu, Congo, to visit the family who ran the orphanage.

---

AS A YOUNG IMMIGRANT BOY from the Netherlands, Ray was curious and inquisitive about the world. He moved to Grand Rapids, Michigan, in his early years. With excitement, he would read through his elementary school library's *National Geographic* magazines, interested in learning about Africa. He wasn't sure what exactly he loved about Africa; all he knew was that he couldn't get enough.

Jayn grew up as a natural nurturer; she spent her childhood babysitting for a woman down the street who was fostering a Black baby. Jayn loved caring for that baby. Jayn later went to a cosmetology school in Grand Rapids in the 1960s, during the civil rights era. One day, the vibrant, gregarious, blond-haired nineteen-year-old was sitting at the back of the city bus while coming home from class one day. At one stop, a Black mother and her child stepped onto the bus; the mother stood toward the front, holding the rail, while her son ran toward the back. With one sudden jerk of the bus, the boy lunged forward and was falling face-first toward the floor. Jayn quickly scooped him up to save him from falling and sat him on her lap. The bus was filled with mostly White passengers who, in unison, inhaled a large gasp and intently watched Jayn playing with the young Black boy. As the mother's stop approached, she and the boy began to exit the bus. Just as the boy was walking out, he quickly turned about and ran back to kiss Jayn on the cheek. More gasps of shock and awe consumed the air of the bus. Jayn didn't think anything of it, but later came to realize a simple gesture of kindness, which transcended race, was a basic act not everyone had the heart to do.

From young ages, both Ray and Jayn were culturally minded and already passionate about breaking societal norms and standing up for racial equity. Ray and Jayn would later meet, marry, and have a family of four children. In 1983, they attended a Christian church, which hosted a weekend mission fair to bring awareness and support to the existing missionaries the church was sponsoring, including one of the main speakers from African Christian Mission. As the speaker presented his mission work in the Congo and showed a map of Africa, the Congo, located right in the middle, began to tug at Jayn's heartstrings. Seeing Congo on the map felt like home to her, although she didn't yet quite understand why. The more she heard about the Congolese people and the work the speaker was doing, the more she just knew her calling was to be a missionary there; however, she was uncertain about how to tell her husband.

Unbeknownst to Jayn, Ray had the same desire. After a mission fair session at their church, Ray came home saying, "I wonder what my parents would think if I told them we were leaving for the Congo." Jayn was enchanted to know Ray was processing the same thing. They asked their children what they thought about moving to the Congo to be missionaries. The children were all immediately excited and on board. Instantly, all their desires, intuition, and purpose converged as if it descended from heaven. A year and a half later, Ray and Jayn and their children were living in the Congo for a three-year missionary commitment.

Within the first year of their mission, the Harkema family visited the orphanage on their days off to spend time with their friends, the Smiths, who were senior missionaries in the organization they belonged to. The Smiths lived in a very small white house next to the orphanage. The house was previously used as the servants' quarters of a Belgian tea plantation. The Congo had been colonized by the Belgians in the late nineteenth century, and was in fact personally owned by the brutal King Leopold II. After intense international pressure, Congo gained independence from Belgium in 1960; as the Belgians moved out of the Congo, the former stables of the tea plantation served as a church and then an orphanage.

Ray and Jayn and their children spent the sunny, warm afternoon with the Smiths. Their youngest children, Eli and Josh, were playing outside with the oldest child, Ted, while Ray, Jayn, and their daughter, Heather, were inside conversing with the Smiths. At one point during the afternoon, Jayn had to use the bathroom, and she weaved through the back of the house and entered through a small bedroom adjacent to the bathroom. As Jayn proceeded into the bedroom, her eyes drew toward a toy doll bassinet placed on the bed. Wrapped inside she saw a bundled-up, tiny brown-skinned doll. Peeking out was the doll's head, the size of a small orange, covered in straight black hair. She immediately thought the doll belonged to Mr. and Mrs. Smith's daughter, Hannah.

After Jayn used the bathroom, her eyes were entranced with the movement of the doll's head. Perplexed, she extended her hand toward the doll. She received quite a surprise to learn the doll was actually a tiny human baby. She looked at the baby in astonishment as her head turned in front of Jayn's very eyes.

As she marveled at the baby's movement, she touched the top of the head—in that moment, she heard a voice inside her say, *Here is your new daughter.*

She was deeply moved and filled with peace as she recognized the still, small voice as God telling her I was hers. Jayn immediately went to Ray and pulled him aside, whispering to him what just happened; he had peace about it as well. Together, Jayn and Ray shared the news with their children and asked what they thought of them adopting me. First to speak was their precocious daughter, Heather, aged fourteen. Heather was eager to bring me home as she thought I was a real live doll she could help take care of. Ted, aged fifteen, was cautious of my sickly condition. Josh, who was eight years old at the time, thought I was small and cute and wanted to take care of me. Eli, aged seven, didn't understand what it meant to bring me home, but he was looking forward to the new adventure. After debriefing with the children and talking about the possibilities, the family had comfort with the powerful message Jayn received.

The Harkemas told the Smiths they wanted to bring me home to care for me. The orphanage workers were worried I wouldn't live to see another day, as they were fearful I could die at any moment. The faith of the Harkema family rose above the fear about my circumstances. Ray and Jayn prayed and had faith in a miracle that I would survive. The very same afternoon, Ray and Jayn became *my* mother and father as they took me into their family and brought me to their home in Bukavu, Congo.

Adoption, especially transracial adoption, is very rare in Bukavu. Children are brought to orphanages to receive care, food, and shelter, not to be adopted. The orphanage I was brought to wasn't an adoption agency. There wasn't any paperwork associated with my arrival and departure from the orphanage; in fact, my adoption wasn't even official at that point. I didn't even have a name. In Bukavu, especially then, in 1985, a White family bringing home a Black baby was extremely rare. Word of mouth spread quickly around the village.

Upon bringing me home, my new family gave me continuous care and love. I was in dire need of medical attention; however, available doctors and operating hospitals were few and far between. My parents gave me medications they were able to get their hands on. For several weeks, they held me, rocked me, cried over me, and prayed for me, while forming a bond with me—through it all, focusing on their faith, believing God's plan was greater than my condition. One day, the youngest child (my new brother), Eli, said, "We have to keep her. We can't let her go back." Even though I wasn't officially a Harkema, I was already in their hearts and part of the family.

Ray's mission work was leading the logistics and construction teams by fixing urgent repairs—vehicles, schools, water supply lines, and a run-down, inoperable hospital in Bukavu. Jayn supported a prison ministry, where she and local women made meals for the region's prisoners to help prevent them from dying of starvation. With the exception of this type of charity, the only way the prisoners were fed was when they were brought outside food from friends or family. Jayn also led a women's ministry, teaching the local women in rural areas the love of God and how to love themselves through the trauma they've experienced.

One day, a German pediatrician came through our village, providing aid to families in need, and she happened to visit with my family. In her satchel, she had a soy-based protein formula that my body was able to digest. Day by day, I started healing and becoming stronger and stronger. A nearby pastor came over to our house, and during the visit, Jayn explained how they were still in need of a name for me and wanted a name with meaning and significance. The pastor picked me up and said, "Like Moses, she was found in the bulrushes by someone who could care for her; her name should be Neema. It's by the grace of God she is alive."

Ray and Jayn were enamored—Neema means "grace" in Swahili. They chose to name me Graci, after the grace of God that I was found. They gave me the middle name Neema to signify God's double grace in my life.

When I was about six months old, my family and I went back to Kidodobo to visit with my biological mother near the orphanage. MariJani, small and frail, with the stature of a teenager, uttered a few words to my mom, amidst nervous, awkward tensions and the struggle of not speaking the same language. She was timid and shy to converse with my White parents, as people from her village didn't often see White people; however, she was happy a family was able to care for me in a way that she wasn't able to. Out of respect for her, my dad paid her family a dowry in honor of the Congolese tradition. If I hadn't been adopted and lived a traditional life with my biological mother, a dowry would have been paid to her from my future husband's family. Since that wasn't going to happen, my mom and dad desired to monetarily honor what MariJani would have received had I lived a healthy life with her. My biological mother gave the blessing to my mom to adopt me. MariJani met my adoptive siblings, as my brother Ted was eager to capture photos of her holding me as she engaged with my mom, to commemorate the impactful day. After that day, we lost contact with MariJani and never heard from her again—because of her frail condition and the violence close to the area, we presumed she died.

My mom and dad knew God had a purpose for me to be a permanent part of their family. They worked tirelessly with the Congolese government to finalize my adoption. My adoption became official when I was one year old. The birth certificate

They chose to name
me Graci, after the grace
of God that I was found.

I received was written in French and had the texture of tissue paper, but that thin, translucent paper paired with my adoption papers resembled the weight of gold and made it possible for me to obtain a Congolese passport. I would later discover that a passport was the key to endless opportunities.

My much older siblings Ted and Heather were in boarding school in Kenya. I didn't spend much time with them during the school year, but when Heather was home, I always clung to her. Josh and Eli looked after me and did everything to protect me. When Josh wasn't looking, I would slip into his Nike shoes, and I felt on top of the world. I thought he was so cool. I wanted to be him. Walking around in his shoes made me feel like I *was* him.

---

MY MEMORIES OF LIVING IN the Congo are vague and initially appear to be random. One memory that sticks out to me was regularly getting my hair braided by a local Congolese woman named Charlotté, who worked for my parents by assisting my mom in the home. Due to high crime rates and theft, it was common for expats to hire locals to stay in the home during the day to help protect the household and land. My mom and dad hired a few locals who became part of the family. Charlotté was tall, elegant, and had a strong presence that commanded the room, perhaps a woman I would one day strive to be. I also remember enjoying watching my dad fix vehicles. I pretended to be like him while carrying toy tools to work on my pretend cars— from a young age, I had been a daddy's girl with a love of cars.

My mom and dad's three-year missionary commitment concluded when my sister Heather was in her last year of boarding school at Rift Valley Academy in Kenya. My parents didn't want to disrupt her senior year, therefore we stayed in Congo until she graduated. I recall her graduation: Heather seemed so proud, and my family was very proud of her; she was a brilliant seventeen-year-old who could speak several languages fluently and had the world as her oyster. We celebrated with delightful European cookies that were served at her graduation. Memories of what I once thought were random occasions without meaning have shown themselves to be compelling first impressions of strong leaders and role models who I've spent much of my life aspiring to be.

I was almost four years old when we began our journey to the United States, specifically a suburb of Grand Rapids, Michigan, where my family lived previously. I was about to embark on the experience of an American education and the opportunity to live the American Dream. I distinctly remember the bumpy, unsettling, turbulent plane ride. I was surrounded with a family of endless love who gave me the world, yet even at a young age, being uprooted and moving across the Atlantic brought a new kind of trauma.

Every season, every decision, every week, every day, every minute, and every second was ordered in the divine timing it needed for God's purpose to defy all of the odds against me. From the time my dad read *National Geographic* magazines, to the day my mom rode on the bus, to the weekend at their church, to the season they moved to Africa, to the week after my birth when MariJani made the crucial decision, to the Wednesday my family chose to visit the orphanage, to the minute my mom had to go to the bathroom, and to the second the German pediatrician came over.

**FACTS ABOUT THE DEMOCRATIC REPUBLIC OF THE CONGO**

Also referred to as the DRC, Congo is a Francophone country, originally colonized by the Belgians in the late 1800s. The DRC is one of the world's richest countries in natural resources, which are estimated to be worth US$24 trillion.

**Geography:** The DRC is the largest country in sub-Saharan Africa. Its landmass is about two-thirds the size of Western Europe. DRC is home to the world's second-largest rainforest. The city of Bukavu borders Rwanda.

**Population:** As of 2021, Bukavu has an estimated urban population of 1,133,000. The population of the DRC is 92 million.

**Climate:** There are two seasons, rainy season and dry season.

**Economy:** The average annual income in the DRC is US$785. In 2019, the United Nations' Human Development Index ranked the DRC as the 175th least-developed country out of 195 countries in the world.

**Common Jobs:** Agriculture—growing and tending to crops—and mining, including copper, cobalt, coltan, diamonds, and gold.

**Popular Foods:** Popular traditional foods are fufu/ugali, cassava leaves, yams, plantains, chicken, fish, and goat meat.

**Languages:** Congo is one of the most linguistically diverse countries in the world, with over two hundred languages spoken in its borders. French, Swahili, Kituba, Lingala, and Tshiluba are the most commonly spoken languages.

**Religions:** Christianity is the most widespread religion, consisting of more than 90 percent of the population. Islam is the second most popular, at less than 5 percent.

----

IN THE MUNDANE MOMENTS, it's often hard for us to see and experience our purpose, or the purpose of others we are surrounded by. What can seem random, ironic, uncanny, or serendipitous can truly be the divine timing of God, the universe, or whatever higher power you may or may not believe in. For me, I believe the order of happenstance occurrences in the early journey of my life was God's intervention and His divine timing.

Are there instances in your life where you felt that the "stars aligned" to assist you in your journey?

# 2

# Learning to Wear the Mask

"There is no greater agony than bearing an untold story inside you."

**MAYA ANGELOU**

**M**Y MOM AND DAD aspired for our family to live the American Dream. My dad's mission in life has always been to love God, love his family, live well, and do well. For him and his parents, moving from the Netherlands to America was the golden ticket—a chance to make dreams come true and live the opportunities his ancestors never had. That is what my parents wanted for me as well.

Education was very important to my mom and dad; upon moving back to the United States from the Congo, the area they chose to live was based on the education system. We moved to a top-rated school district, which was one of their most important aspects of living the American Dream. My two oldest siblings moved away to college and quickly settled into their adult lives with degrees, marriages, kids, and careers, while my other two siblings were embarking on their teenage years.

We lived in a homogenous, non-diverse suburban area in Grand Rapids, Michigan. Our block was quiet, with four houses of different architectural styles and decent-sized yards, surrounded by lush greenery and tall trees. We moved onto five acres of land with a large Victorian-style home, which my mom decided to have painted carnation pink with violet trim... talk about making an entrance! Our neighbors adjacent to us were a family with five children. Their oldest child, Linden, was a girl my age who also went to my school, and we quickly became best friends. Other neighbors on our street were a couple with one son about thirteen or fourteen years older than me who became friends with my brothers. Our other neighbors next to us were an older married couple. They had a pool, so naturally they were a hit with us kids.

A lot of my brothers' time was consumed with friends, work, sports, and band practice; therefore, they didn't spend much time at home anymore. Much of my time outside of school was spent with my mom, dad, and my neighborhood friends.

It was important to my mom that I embrace my African culture and keep it present in my appearance. She pulled my short, tightly curled, coarse hair into small pigtails with beads and barrettes on top of my head and dressed me in long colorful dresses or floral tops. For me, having an African appearance and living in my new world was too much, and I hated those frilly dresses. When I began elementary school, I immediately felt like I stuck out. I was a brown-skinned African among a sea of blond-haired, blue-eyed kids. On my first day at my new school, I became known as "the Black girl." In my neighborhood, in my school, and at my church, most often the only Black female face I saw was in the mirror. Because I didn't look like the other kids, everyone knew who I was.

I promptly learned to be outgoing and play sports to look like I was fitting in, even though I didn't feel like it. Any sport with a ball was my favorite sport. Even though I wasn't comfortable on the inside, *I have to act like it*, I thought. I didn't want others to know I felt like I didn't belong. I was fortunate to have an outgoing, social personality, which allowed for making friends easily. I quickly traded in my beaded pigtails and color-ful dresses for black Jordan's and oversized Nike T-shirts while rocking a mini Afro.

---

EVEN SURROUNDED BY MY LOVING FAMILY and my new-found friends, I still felt like I was in the wrong place. I hated not looking like anyone else in my new life. My early years had been the opposite. I didn't know how to tell my family how I was feeling. I thought, *How dare I tell them I feel like I don't fit in, when I'm grateful just to have breath?* The culture shock of feeling like I was the only one of my kind was a challenge I was not equipped for. I was perceived as one of the nice girls who many kids wanted to be friends with; however, internally, I was torn apart. I longed to see someone else who looked like me—I longed to look like one of them.

Some of the students in my school were more cultured than others, while other students would ask me questions like, "Why are you Black?" and "Why is your skin so dark?" My earliest memories of my identity were the moments I had to defend what I looked like and who I was. I felt as if something was wrong with *me*.

My dad was and *is* a hard worker and entrepreneur; he has always loved taking care of the family and making sure we all had everything we needed while living under his roof. My mom was a stay-at-home mom. She was often found volunteering at my school library, attending my school events, volunteering at church functions, painting and creating in her art studio, and entertaining with picnics and tea parties. When Friday came around, my mom, dad, and I all had an extra skip in our steps. Friday meant payday, and it also meant my mom, dad, and I would go out for dinner at one of our favorite local restaurants nearby. My mom is a gourmet cook, and growing up, I was a very picky eater, which meant I was overjoyed and pounced at the opportunity to order whatever food I wanted at the restaurants, which always included simple foods like chicken fingers and french fries—foods my gourmet-chef mom wouldn't make at home.

One particular Friday evening, my mom, dad, and I went to a casual American restaurant close to our neighborhood. My dad held open the door as my mom entered the restaurant with me trailing in closely behind her as we headed inside. The three of us stood in front of the host stand, and the host asked, "How many?" My dad quickly responded, "Three." The host, a White woman in her late teens or early twenties, looked down at me and questioned, "Are you with them?"

I hesitated in confusion, turning my head slightly to the side to look at her. "Yes?" I said as if I was questioning her right back.

I looked up at my dad, he nodded yes, and we started to follow the host to our table. I sat in the booth, wondering why the host asked if I was with them. I looked back toward the host stand and thought, *Does she think I am with a different family?* I was puzzled; there weren't any other families there... there wasn't anybody else there. *Does she think I, a young kid, am going out to eat by myself?* I was so baffled, hurt even, but my mom and dad didn't seem outwardly phased by the host's question, which puzzled me even more. I didn't know what to do or what to say, so I just let it go.

About a year or two later at another restaurant, it happened again, and again another time after that, and most recently just a few years ago. My thought was always, *Why doesn't the host think I belong with my family?* Each time it happened, my mom and dad didn't seem bothered by the question and each time, as upset as it made me, I had no idea what to say other than, "Yes, I'm with them."

Ignorance in human behavior can unfortunately show up as microaggressions, whether intentionally or unintentionally. A microaggression or micro-behavior is "the act of discriminating against a marginalized group by means of comments or actions." It is "a subtle but offensive comment or action directed at a member of a marginalized group, especially a racial minority, that is often unintentionally offensive or unconsciously reinforces a stereotype." I don't believe the hosts intended to discriminate against me, but their ignorance of our family structure, in conjunction with the representation of our family, didn't align with their expectations, which resulted in microaggressions.

Microaggressions can be subtle. Typically, the marginalized person, me in this case, feels the microaggression strongly—it feels as if I'm being called out—and the non-marginalized group, my parents, may not recognize the behavior as a microaggression because it doesn't always personally affect them.

---

AS EARLY AS KINDERGARTEN, I spent many mornings watching my mom getting ready for the day. She didn't leave the house until she was fully ready, glammed from head to toe. She had the same routine each morning: facial cleanser followed by foundation, eye makeup, and then finished with her hair. She had rows of makeup and skin care products that were in drawers at my eye level in the bathroom. I would look up at the shade of my mom's foundation, then I would look down at my hand and look back up at the makeup, noticing the vastly different shades between the two. Unanswered questions flooded my inquisitive mind, *Why can't my skin be light like hers? Why am I so different? Why can't I look like her?*

I increasingly began to feel ashamed of my smooth, milk chocolate–shaded, melanin skin. When I didn't think my mom and dad were paying attention, I snuck into my mom's makeup drawer and smeared the beige-colored foundation onto my face. I continued to do it until my face was fully covered. Looking into my reflection in the mirror, I then grabbed a tan-colored bath towel from the adjacent bathroom drawer and draped it over my head, pretending it was my long blond hair. I stared into my reflection in the mirror, curling in my full lips, making them look flat; I contentedly and peacefully gazed at the image looking back at me. I thought that's what I was supposed to look like. In that siloed moment, I felt like I belonged—yet I was all alone, locked in the bathroom.

Appearing so different from everyone else made me *feel* so different from everyone else. Out of fear of not wanting to be even more different from others, there were secrets I began to keep from the world. At the age of six, I knew I was attracted to girls. My first crush was a girl in my first-grade class. Her eyes sparkled like light-blue diamonds and during recess I would watch her long blond hair blow in the wind as her earrings twinkled in the sunlight. She was tender and sweet, and when she said hi to me, it was as if nothing else mattered—my face lit up and my stomach flooded with butterflies.

On school afternoons before a holiday, we often had movie days, where the students in the class would pull large beanbags toward the corner of the room. We would pile on top of the beanbags to watch whichever movie the teacher selected for us. On one movie day, several of the boys wanted to sit on a beanbag near my crush. Some of the boys would push each other in order to get closer to her. I saw the boys poke at her and

Appearing so different
from everyone else made
me *feel* so different from
everyone else.

flirt with her—I was jealous and sad; I wished I could be them. I wished I could be the one poking the side of her upper arm and bashfully snickering afterwards, but I knew that wasn't going to happen because I wasn't a boy. As children, we think our crush is the center of our universe. I wanted to tell her that I liked her, but the risk of losing her or my other friends was too much, so I knew I could never tell her... I could never tell anyone.

On the playground, my friends and I would play princess on top of the slide, pretending that we were trapped in a castle, and we would need a prince to come rescue us. I played the game because that's what my friends wanted to do; however, I never wanted a prince to rescue me. I never wanted a prince; I secretly wanted to be the prince rescuing the pretty princesses. Out of fear that my friends would find out that I liked girls, I pretended to like boys. When I had who-is-your-crush conversations with my friends, I pretended to be straight and substituted my crush's name and the butterflies she gave me with names like Nick, Nathan, and Derek. I didn't want my friends to have reason to think I liked girls, so I giggled along with them about the boys all of the other girls thought were cute.

I instinctively thought that if I shared my truth of being gay, I wouldn't be loved or accepted. Almost daily, my mom would tell me about God's purpose in my life and that God created me to be beautifully and wonderfully made. I didn't believe that God made mistakes, but I wondered why He made me gay, and many times I tried to pray away the gay. I didn't think anyone would understand, and I didn't want people to think I was different. I just wanted to be like everyone else. I already looked different from everyone in my life, and being gay on top of that meant I *was* different from everyone else I knew.

I had a belief that being LGBTQ+ (let me explain, as a six-year-old, I only knew the word *gay*) meant I wasn't going to be loved and I would be shunned from others. As early as we can form consciousness, we are able to form unconscious or implicit biases. We all have biases as a part of human nature. Bias is "a prejudice in favor of or against one thing, person, or group." Biases are our immediate thoughts or opinions about someone or something—it's the first thought or association that pops into our mind. Some biases are innate, while others stem from stereotypes, past experiences, information we have seen in the media, or opinions or rumors from others that have been passed down generationally, systematically, and institutionally.

Nobody ever told me being gay or LGBTQ+ was wrong. I never explicitly heard anything negative about LGBTQ+ people; however, it had already been ingrained in me through family, friends, church, media, and society that *someday* I would need to fall in love with a man, get married, and have kids, or that someday I would find the right person for me, and that person would be a man, or someday I would find my prince. My world didn't consist of any representation of others who were LGBTQ+, so I truly thought I was the only one, and feeling like the only one felt wrong, as though I was wrong. Even though I had loving friends and family, I couldn't jeopardize losing people in my life. Somehow, I thought if people knew about my crush or knew that I liked girls instead of boys, they wouldn't understand, my friends would think I was weird, or my family wouldn't want me to be in their family anymore. Being me and letting others know who I was felt like a risk that was far too great—I couldn't disappoint them; I couldn't lose them; I couldn't let them know.

As an adoptee who was brought to a new world, I couldn't risk abandonment or rejection, so I learned how to keep secrets and make it appear like I fit in. Being similar to my friends and going along with the expectations others had of me gave me a false yet less-anxiety-ridden and semi-comforting sense of security and acceptance. Adoptees, especially as children, often develop a fear of rejection or fear abandonment after being uprooted from their birth family. Safety and security are very important for those who have been adopted. Speaking the truth of who I was could risk *everything* that felt comfortable to me.

I hid my truth about my sexual orientation from most of the people in my life for *twenty-two years*, and that's a really long time to keep a secret. During all those years, I piled on mask after mask—masks hiding my true identity, much more than my mother's beige foundation could. I believed I had to look the part and be just like everyone else to have friends and feel accepted. We often force ourselves to learn how to wear a mask—a mask that limits who we really are to fit into social situations, certain groups, friends, family, religions, and work-place environments.

Many of us have experienced aspects of our lives or identi-ties that make us feel like we're alone. We feel like we are the only ones to exist—we think nobody would understand. We have entire dialogs in our heads about the dichotomy between our true selves and who we are expected to be. We believe the avoidance of speaking the truth and the avoidance of being our authentic selves and often cave under the pressure to mimic societal norms as a form of self-preservation—a type of self-preservation that can help makes us feel safe and accepted, even if we are living a lie.

Whether we are six or sixty years old, many of us often cover parts of our identities due to our conceived and perceived biases. Legal scholar and author Kenji Yoshino defines covering as "downplaying aspects of our identity that make us differ-ent from mainstream society." I started covering in elementary

Covering is an action that often follows underrepresented and marginalized children from the playground to the boardroom.

school. Covering is an action that often follows underrepresented and marginalized children from the playground to the boardroom. We see and experience covering in the workplace without even realizing it.

Yoshino states, "Covering in the workplace is the act of concealing something about oneself to avoid making other people feel uncomfortable or to lessen attention to a given characteristic." In the workplace, people often cover their background, ethnicity, identity, religion, mental health, physical disabilities, sexual orientation, marital status, veteran status, familial status, and other identities. In Yoshino's book *Covering: The Hidden Assault on Our Civil Rights*, he reports 61 percent of participants in his research study cover at work. Participants who reported covering in the workplace include 83 percent of LGBTQ+ people, 81 percent of people with physical or mental disabilities, 79 percent of Blacks, 67 percent of women of color, 66 percent of women, 63 percent of Latinx, 61 percent of Asian Americans and Pacific Islanders, and 45 percent of straight, White males. Forty percent of those who cover reported that covering gave them a negative sense of self. Covering commonly serves as our self-preservation for social acceptance and security. And yet... it also hurts us.

As children, teenagers, and adults, we take feelings of being different or isolated as something wrong with us. We often think and believe *we* are the problem, and instead of seeking the root cause of our discomfort, we perpetuate and torment ourselves to our own detriment. I was too afraid to take the risk of not wearing the mask when I was young. Learning what type of support and power I had was going to take much more time to learn.

## IDENTITY EXERCISE

I incorporate this exercise in my "Embracing Diversity, Overcoming Bias & Rising in Inclusion" training workshops. Have something to take notes with if that's accessible.

Write down five attributes of your identity. It can be anything. When you think of yourself, what do you think of? How do you identify? It can be identities like parent, spouse, religion, appearance, gender identity, sexual orientation, race, career, personality traits, etc. After you have written down the top five attributes of your identity, read them to yourself.

Looking at your list, physically cross out two of them. It can be any two. Now, cross out one more. Between the remaining two attributes, cross out one more. You have one attribute left. How was that experience?

Was it challenging? Did it feel limiting? Do you feel guilty? Did it feel like you were crossing out parts of yourself? Did it feel like you were ranking which aspects of yourself were most important?

All of those experiences you may have had during the exercise—being challenged and torn, feeling guilty and limited, and ranking parts of yourself—are experiences we have when we feel the need to wear a mask just to fit in, go to school, come to work, or feel accepted. It's challenging, it's uncomfortable, and it's limiting.

The moment we had at the beginning of the exercise, reading the five attributes, almost felt redundant. You may have thought, *Yeah, that's me in a nutshell if I have to narrow myself down to five things.* That moment of being at ease reading our attributes, that's the feeling of authenticity—to show up and project how we think and feel as ourselves.

We wear masks when we don't feel safe or supported; the mask resembles protection from others learning the true attributes of who we are. As proactive as it can feel in the moment, deep down it's exhausting and scary to need a mask in the first place. The feeling of crossing out identities of who are we, just to fit in—that's how we feel when we aren't in an inclusive environment, when we have to hang up parts of ourselves just to walk through the door.

It's important that we learn to see ourselves, and others, not just for the one identity remaining, but for all of the identities that make us who we are, so we can learn to live without the mask.

---

WE ALL GO THROUGH JOURNEYS in our lives where we feel like we're alone. The truth is, we aren't alone; we just don't always feel brave enough to share our experiences and identities of our true selves. With support, we have the incredible power to rise and overcome these adversities, fears, challenges, and masks that cover who we authentically are. We are more resilient than we think—we just can't always see it.

# 3

# Violation and Liberation

"And still I rise."

**MAYA ANGELOU**

LATER IN elementary school, I had become quite the social butterfly and established my core group of friends. One afternoon at school, my friends and I were outside on the playground at recess playing catch. I threw the ball to a White, brown-haired boy who I thought I was friends with. Shortly after I threw the ball, he called me nigger. Immediately, the other students looked directly at me and gasped in surprise. I didn't know what the word meant. I had never heard that word before. It was as if the students, my friends, were frozen in place, witnessing something that they knew was bad and inappropriate but didn't have the ability to tell me why it was inappropriate, nor did they say to the boy that it was wrong.

One of the teachers working the recess shift was called over by one of the students, and that student repeated what was said. The teacher separated me from the boy. The teacher frantically asked me if I was okay and nervously exclaimed, "I'm sorry that happened!" After seeing how scared the students were and the panic on the teacher's face, I realized that what the boy called me was something bad, something derogatory, something awful. After being separated from my friends, the teacher told us we had to stop playing. I felt like I was the one who did something wrong. Everyone was scared and silent and looking at me. All I wanted to do was just keep playing with my friends. I wondered, *Am I being punished for a bad word someone said to me? Why can't we keep playing?*

After we came in from recess, all the kids kept talking about what happened, about what the boy had said to me. I heard whispers as we went back to our classroom. I realized the whispers about what happened were because of the color of my skin. The whispers were because of me, the Black girl. It was my first serious encounter with overt racism. The boy said that because of how I looked. He called me that word because of *my* skin, because my skin didn't look like his skin, because my skin didn't look like *anyone's* skin. As the afternoon continued, a sadness came over me. I sat at my desk looking shamefully at my brown hands; I hated how they looked; I hated the color, so I put my hands in my pockets so I couldn't see them.

When I arrived home from school, I told my mom what happened. She told me what the word meant. She also told me that I was beautiful and that I was created in God's image. She tried to be comforting, but I didn't grasp her words. I spaced out into what felt like darkness. I knew my friends wouldn't look at me the same way; they wouldn't see me like they saw themselves.

When the boy called me that word, he might not have known what it meant. He more than likely didn't hear that word from another kid, more probable is that he heard it from an adult.

He said something bad to me because of who I am, not because of who he is or what he was taught. I don't know what the teacher or my friends said to the boy, but I do know our friendship dissolved after that day. Because the next day, everyone acted as if nothing ever happened.

When we are in a position of authority or privilege, we have an opportunity to be an ally. When we witness an injustice against another person because of their identity, we have an opportunity to be empathetic and kind. We also have an ability and responsibility to be a voice and use our platform to call out discrimination and help implement change. A grandiose gesture is not (always) required: "That's not cool," "That's not right," "We don't use that language here," or "That's not funny" can go a long way. Your voice is powerful. Sometimes, all it takes is one person to say something, one person to speak up. Being an ally means showing support, listening, being present, speaking up, meeting people where they are, being in tune, and checking in on the mental health and well-being of others.

---

ON DAYS THAT MY BROTHERS were home after school, sometimes another guy in the neighborhood would come over to hang out with them. I loved being able to hang around my brothers, since I didn't spend as much time with them. I was into anything that my brothers were into. Their friend was in his late teens or early twenties. Since we lived on five acres of land, my brothers sure learned how to utilize all the space. We had fun on dirt bikes, snowmobiles, and a three-wheeler, and my brothers would build jumps for our bikes and shoot targets in the backyard. I would sled down a hill in the backyard in the winter. We all spent a lot of time outside.

One afternoon after school, the neighborhood guy came over when my brothers weren't home. My mom was volunteering at a function, and my dad was at work. The neighbor told me he wanted to show me a trail he found deep in the woods.

With excitement, I was eager to see it. We walked for what felt like quite a while. I kept asking where the trail was, and he would say, "We are almost there. We have to keep walking."

He was tall and lanky, and with each step he took with his long legs, my short legs scurried to take three steps just to catch up. We kept walking, and then he stopped. We were surrounded by tall trees. I couldn't see my house anymore, I couldn't hear any cars on the street, and I couldn't hear anything else, just the rustle of the leaves on the trees. Nothing looked familiar; all I could see were tall trees in every direction. The neighbor asked me to come close to him. Without hesitation, I took a step closer.

Then his playful demeanor became very stern. He told me to take my pants off. I thought it was a strange request, but I did it. He then demanded, "Take off your panties."

My body immediately felt stiff, the confrontation was overwhelming, consuming. I looked at him in discomfort and despair. He told me if I didn't do it, he would tell everyone it was my fault, and he would hurt my family. Reluctantly, I took my underwear off. He forced me onto the ground, until I was lying on pine needles. He grabbed my skinny frame tightly, then moved his face between my legs, and then inserted himself inside me. I was paralyzed; I could barely breathe. I thought I was screaming at the top of my lungs, but no sound was coming out. Nobody could hear me. I couldn't use my voice.

He grabbed my face and threatened that if I told anyone, horrible things would happen to me. I was nine years old... deflated... powerless.

———————

THE NEIGHBOR KEPT COMING OVER, and when my parents weren't home or when my brothers were elsewhere, it continued to happen again and again and again, and each time he was more stern and angrier than the time before. Then afterwards, he would be playful, as if nothing ever happened. It was like it was a game to him, to see what he could do to me without getting caught.

When I was eleven, it happened in my own home, in the same room as my family. My brothers were watching a movie: the lights were off, the room was dark, and he had me behind the couch. I don't believe anyone knew we were there. He covered my mouth and pinned me down so I wouldn't make a sound. For years, he took my power; he threatened me; he threatened me with my family. I couldn't let something happen to them; I couldn't have them think this was my fault; I couldn't have them be disappointed in me. I handed over my control. I didn't know what else to do. I was helpless and numb; he took my innocence; he took part of me. *What would my parents think? What would my brothers think?*

I was plummeting down in a spiral, and I didn't know how to make it stop. I didn't know how to get out. I was filled with anger and guilt. *Why am I here? Why is this happening to me?* I had never heard of this happening to anybody else before. My shame led me to believe I was the only one this was happening to, that I was the only one of my kind. I knew there had to be a reason why I was chosen to live, but I didn't know what it was or why I was living this life. I couldn't talk to anybody, so I remained in my head, reliving the moments and also imagining I was somebody else.

I believed the illusion that silence was *safety*. I thought my silence would protect my family and also me.

A few months later in the summer, when I was between fifth and sixth grade, he asked me to take off my shorts. I did. He asked me to take off my panties. I took them off and threw them at him. Then I quickly put my shorts back on and I sprinted into my house and locked the door. I didn't know that was going to be the last time he would try to molest me. Shortly after, he and his family moved away.

I mourned my life before him. I remained haunted by the thought of him every single day, worried he would show up at my school, come to our house, or that I would see him in a public place. Dread and paranoia forced me to avoid the woods and always look behind me when I walked, in case he crept up next to me. I was in a constant state of fear and angst. I was tormented by the belief that I couldn't use my voice. I believed if I spoke about it, my family would hurt from knowing my pain. I didn't want my family to go through that kind of pain. I was full of embarrassment, and I felt ashamed.

For nearly ten years, I kept silent about what he did to me. Then, when I was in my mid-twenties, I received a text from an old neighbor friend. The text was an image that contained the neighbor's smug mug shot; he was out of state and behind bars. He had been sentenced to five consecutive life sentences in prison after being convicted of ten charges involving sexual conduct with a minor under the age of twelve, sexual abuse, aggravated assault, and child molestation involving three young girls in his neighborhood.

I believed the illusion that silence was *safety*. I thought my silence would protect my family and also me. Sometimes, we don't even realize what is happening; trauma can slip in through a crack. Whether it's on the playground or in the boardroom, we doubt ourselves, we lose track of our confidence and who we are. Others speak for us, parts of ourselves are taken, and we often think we can't get it back or get *us* back. When others speak for us, our power is taken away—we lose ourselves and become distanced from our true self and purpose. Typically, it happens slowly—one comment, microaggression, or violation at a time—perhaps when we are trying to please somebody, accomplish something, or simply fit in, when a violator just sneaks up and takes it... takes us. We tend to give those who make us feel inferior a pass. We say it's okay just to cover up our own discomfort or our own vulnerabilities. We believe that if we don't think about it or give the violation attention, then maybe it didn't happen. Maybe if we don't talk about it, we can forget it. We might even do a good job of keeping silent and pretending for as long as we are able to, but it's time we take our voices back.

---

AS A DISTRACTION FROM THE TRAUMA, the isolation, and the silence, I immersed myself in as many sports as I could. I bounced into basketball, swung into softball, spiked into volleyball, ran a dash of track, continued down the field to soccer, and ultimately kicked into Division One men's varsity football. Harnessing my energy on the field and on the court was a way to feel like I was a part of something, to feel like I belonged, like I was on a team.

Early on in my soccer days, my dad encouraged me to be a goalie. It was a terrifying position that none of the girls wanted to do. My dad told me all I had to do was catch the ball. It sounded simple, catch the ball, and then kick it out— and it was also an opportunity where I could skip out on all of that running? I was sold. My athleticism carried me into high school. I went to a large Division One high school with about two thousand students, about five hundred students in each grade. The district prioritized sports, and even more so, they prioritized winning. We had a decent soccer program and an even better football program as former state champions.

Each year during homecoming week, the girls would play in an all-female Powder Puff game, juniors versus seniors. I was a junior. Since I was a goalie in soccer, the team thought I was a natural fit to be our kicker. I had never kicked a football before. We did a coin toss, I kicked the football to the back of the end zone, the crowd roared, and the refs, who were also the men's varsity coaches, all did doubletakes. I wasn't sure what it meant. Was that where I was supposed to kick the ball? Apparently, it was a good kick. We scored and I kicked the ball again, same thing. After the game the refs pulled me aside and asked me if I would be interested in trying out to play on the men's varsity team the next year as their existing kicker was graduating. I chuckled at the question and responded with something along with lines of, "Thanks, but no thanks."

I was sixteen, I had grown out of my tomboy phase, and was into makeup and high heels. A woman had never played on my school's men's varsity football team before. Many had attempted, but all had failed. As a closeted queer, I couldn't do something as audacious as play men's football and have my cover blown, or so I thought. I was well known in my school. I mean, of course *everyone* knew the Black girl. Out of the five hundred students, I was one of the only Black girls in my grade. For a lot of my friends, I was their only Black friend, so all of my words and actions became their conceptions of all Black people, outside of the celebrities we saw on TV. I felt like eyes were always watching me—what I would say, what things I would do, how I would look. I made sure my mom took me clothes shopping at only the trendiest stores; fortunately, she often rewarded me with new shoes for good grades and good behavior. My mom was also thrilled at the opportunity to take me makeup shopping at MAC Cosmetics, at that time one of the few stores that carried my foundation shade, and I was thrilled to be able to shop with her after all those years of watching her put on makeup. With my friends, I pretended to crush on all the cute boys because I still didn't want to risk anyone knowing my orientation. I was girly; I was feminine; everyone thought I was straight. I couldn't dare play men's varsity football. *What would people say? What would people think?*

Word of my lengthy kick into the end zone at the Powder Puff game spread throughout the school. Everyone was talking about it—the students and the teachers. Before I knew it, I was having encouraging conversations with my dad about how me playing football could create an impact in our city. I started practicing with the team my junior year. My dad even built me a field goal post in our front yard so I could practice at home. My after-school routine was weightlifting with the guys, then football conditioning, right to women's soccer practice, then coming home to kick in the front yard until it was too dark for me to see where the footballs landed. I went to every football camp during the summer and attended every two-a-day and three-a-day practices.

Senior year had arrived. When fall came, I tried out and officially made the team. The head football coach, Coach Sig, was one of my biggest supporters. He was a tough guy, bald head and goatee, a man of few words, but when he spoke, everyone listened. He saw my kicking potential and combatted anyone who tried to protest me being on the team. He believed I earned the right to play, and he let everyone who questioned him know that. He advocated for me with the school board and even stuck up for me with all of the football dads who were jealous of the media attention that I was getting and their sons weren't getting.

I was under a lot of pressure to perform; emotionally, the pressure was taxing at times, and I felt the weight of the city cheering me on, compounding on my shoulders. I didn't want to let anyone down. I didn't want to let myself down. I found something I did uniquely well: my longest field goal in practice was forty yards. The average NFL field goal distances range between thirty-five and fifty yards. I exerted every part of me to harness my skill. The season was intense! Thank goodness I had just played soccer the season prior, which kept me in good shape to keep up with the guys during all of the drills.

We had to dress up and wear our jerseys on Friday game days. My dad dropped me off at school on Friday mornings, and I would wear black heels, black dress pants, and my number seven maroon jersey, welcoming the sight of uplifting, glitter-filled signs taped to my locker and freshly baked cookies from the pretty cheerleaders. I always blushed when I saw the cheerleaders on game days—some of them were close friends and some of my biggest fans. Occasionally, on Friday afternoons, local TV news crews would come pull me out of class to interview me for the five o'clock news before the game. I loved when the news crews came, but my new small-town fame made it hard for me to tell who my real friends were and who were those trying to get a jumpstart on their future broadcasting career by making a cameo appearance on my news story.

During my freshman year, a brand-new mall opened across the street from my high school. During senior year, my close friends Jen, Tim, and I would go to the mall for lunch. A common occurrence at the mall would be young girls with their suburban stay-at-home mothers, asking for my autograph. The girls would tell me they wanted to grow up and play football just like me. I didn't realize what them seeing me did for their hopes and aspirations. By senior year, I was no longer referred to as "the Black girl." I was simply known as the first woman in Grandville Public Schools' history to play men's varsity football.

Our team went to the playoffs, and our team photo hung on the wall at the local Applebee's. I appreciated my new identity and my escape from my internal turmoil. Finding resilience through my new identity became my liberation from the violation I had experienced earlier.

Our resilience can serve as an outlet or an escape from something more painful, something we are covering up, or something we feel incapable of dealing with. The greatest act of resilience is simply not giving up. I learned to rise from pain and fear and transcend into movement and strength. I didn't yet know how to use my voice; however, I learned to treat and view my body as a force instead of something broken. Playing football didn't heal me from my trauma, but it saved my life. It helped me get to know a different part of me that I didn't know existed. Doing something that nobody else had ever done before, such as being the first woman to join the men's varsity football team at my school, gave me the hope that my life wasn't over and that I had more to live for and an opportunity to create an impact for others.

## WHAT'S YOUR STORY?

We all have a story. My journey in writing my story started by journaling. Writing about how I was dealing with challenging and intense moments was the only way I was able to process those moments. In your journal, or whatever you take notes on, really think about who you are and the path you've taken. You can write as much or as little as feels comfortable for you. You can start here, and if you find yourself in the flow, go with it! If you find yourself stumped, come back to it. I didn't come back to my story until almost five years after I started writing it. Here are some prompts to get you started.

- How do you think of yourself?

- Where are you from?

- What are you most passionate about?

- What is your family like?

- What are a couple events from your life you recall had a real impact on you?

- What traits make you unique?

- Think about a time you faced adversity but were able to overcome it. What happened and how did you feel afterwards?

- What do you wish people knew about you?

- What is your mission statement in life?

- What would you like your legacy to be?

———————

BEING THE ONLY FEMALE, the only LGBTQ+, the only Black, the only immigrant, the only adoptee, the only survivor, the only you-name-it ... can feel isolating and exhausting, but it's also an opportunity to let others know it is possible for them, too, and that there is much more to you than what meets their eye. Because of our identities, many of us have countless barriers and biases, stigmas and stereotypes, labels and limitations placed on us. The ceiling will never shatter until someone breaks it. Is there a ceiling you're ready to shatter?

# 4

# The Oscar-Worthy Role

"Everyone is insecure.
I think, really, it comes
from… a desire to want
to be in control of how
you're represented."

**LAVERNE COX**

IN 2003, after high school graduation, I got accepted to attend Grand Valley State University nearby. I was determined to go to that university since fourth grade. I had always looked up to my sister, since she graduated from there, so it was a no-brainer for me that I was going to go there as well. One of the things I was most excited about for college was no longer being one of the few Black people. When I arrived at college, I was welcomed with the expectation of no longer being the only Black person in the room. The school had focused heavy recruiting efforts in the Metro Detroit and Chicago areas, and as a result, brought in many more Black and Brown faces than I was used to seeing. Sometimes, there were up to five Black people in my classes and I would also see many Black, Brown, Asian American and Pacific Islander, and Indigenous students walking around campus. It was everything I longed for; it was amazing.

At the age of eighteen, I had obtained US Permanent Residency, which provided my green card and the ability to work. My adoption was official in 1986, when I was one year old, but as I was adopted by US citizens who were living in the Congo at the time, I was not grandfathered US citizenship. That didn't become a law until years after my adoption. I had to go through the laborious, attorney-intensive, expensive US naturalization process as an immigrant. I had an eye for expensive things, and being a recent green card holder, which now allowed me to work, I was eager to be a part of the workforce and begin making my own money. I started my first job as a sales associate at the Gap.

I had a fascination with downtown city life, blazers, and skyscrapers. In my early years of college, in between classes, I would drive to Grand Valley State University's downtown Grand Rapids campus, walk the streets, memorize the buildings, and, more importantly, recognize the names on those buildings, googling who those people were, and who ran those companies. As an eighteen-year-old, dressed in my nicest business attire outfit, I would walk through the downtown buildings with confidence a mile high, envisioning myself working in those buildings.

One particular day, in my second year of college, I visited one of my mom's church friends who worked at one of the large law firms in downtown Grand Rapids. Enthusiasm filled me as I took the elevator to the top floor. I arrived at the reception desk to be greeted by my mom's friend. The view from the seventeenth floor overlooked the city. At the time, there were only two other buildings in Grand Rapids that were taller. Gazing out the window, I felt like I was standing on top of the world. My mom's friend proudly introduced me to her colleagues. I greeted them and returned firm handshakes and an intentional look in the eye with everyone I met. She said something along the lines of, "You should work were. You could be a messenger." I had no idea what that meant, but I knew I'd like to be a professional working in a tall glass building in between undergrad classes.

I interviewed with the human resources department of the law firm and had an instant rapport with the HR manager. She knew who I was from my football days, as her daughter and I went to high school together and ran track together in previous years. Within a few weeks and a couple of interviews, I got the job, juggling full-time school, a part-time job at the Gap, and now a part-time messenger role at the law firm, which I soon found out meant delivering mail to the attorneys, being a processes server, serving subpoenas and restraining orders, and doing court filings at courthouses throughout Michigan. Being in my late teens, I found the work thrilling. I felt like a detective on *Law & Order*. I was the one to hand deliver court-issued paperwork of warrants, testimony requests or summons of those being sued or being witness to someone being sued, divorced, or involved in situations such as custody battles or personal protection orders, and say, "You've been served."

After a few years of working at the law firm, I was promoted to a receptionist, and I helped assist the marketing and client services departments for high-profile events. I was making $8.50 an hour, living with roommates, making a total of $25,000 a year between both jobs. I resembled the starving college student you hear about. Most of my colleagues were at least fifteen to twenty years older than me. On many occasions, I couldn't even afford to buy toilet paper, and I certainly couldn't afford to buy groceries. In the mornings after I woke up, I peed in the shower. If I had to go number two, I had to hold it until I got to work. When I arrived at work, I would stuff some squares of toilet paper into my pocket to bring home for the evening. The firm provided bagels for the office on Monday mornings. I always discreetly took two—one for lunch and another to bring home for dinner. The little money that I did have was spent on rent, fixing my car, and buying new clothes from the business section at the Gap with my 50 percent discount.

I was determined to not "look" like I didn't have much money. Even if I only had a dollar to my name, my clothes were always pressed, and my appearance was always fresh and put together. Our society is so quick to judge based on appearance. I believed if I looked poor, or didn't look professional and presentable, nobody would take me seriously. I spent a lot of time getting ready every day, not because I was vain, but because I wanted to be seen and valued.

I quickly built strong relationships with my colleagues, and many of them took me under their wings and became my mentors. My social, confident personality was very beneficial in networking and building relationships with many of the attorneys and legal secretaries. Spending time with them gave me the opportunity to learn about corporate America and the power of networking much earlier than many of my peers. I wasn't afraid to ask the attorneys and legal secretaries whom I had close relationships with to lunch. I picked up on their cues and learned to mimic their behaviors and terminology, while increasing my business acumen—and at the same time I got a free lunch, because they always paid the bill.

I offered to work at every firm-sponsored, high-profile event that I could, which meant time and a half for pay, a free meal, a glass or two of wine, and networking opportunities with some of the city's most influential leaders, movers, and shakers. A few times, I was photographed in a suit, standing in a boardroom or leaning next to a conference table, for the landing page of the law firm's website. It appeared that my image on the website was a way for the firm to mitigate their lack of ethnic diversity. At the events, numerous leaders from the community mentioned they recognized me from the website. I felt a lot of pressure to perform well. I was one of two Black people working at the firm at the time, one of the youngest employees, and the daughter of my colleague's friend. There were great expectations placed on me.

My inability to be authentic hindered my ability to climb the corporate ladder.

My inability to be authentic hindered my ability to climb the corporate ladder. I believed if I worked and lived to meet the great expectations of my bosses and colleagues, I would be "qualified" for promotions. At that age, what I knew of success was everything that my colleagues and my parents were. I strived to follow in their footsteps. But I felt like the token at the law firm. At one point, I even planned on going to law school to become a lawyer, and I spent months studying for the LSAT. A freak accident of being run over by a car kept me from going to law school, but I'll get to that later.

At the law firm, I was surrounded by many folks who had an opinion of how I should live my life. Common questions and remarks I received from my colleagues were, "Why aren't you seeing someone?" "I'm surprised some guy hasn't snatched you up." "You're pretty, why don't you have a boyfriend?" as if my level of attractiveness was synonymous with my worthiness of a boyfriend. At the time in Michigan and in more than twenty-five other states, it was legal to be fired from your job and evicted from your home for being LGBTQ+. I couldn't risk losing my job or losing my home if someone found out, so I continued to bury my secret. My fear of rejection kept me from wanting to risk losing approval from my coworkers.

---

FEELING THE PRESSURE AND EXPECTATIONS from my colleagues, I pretended that I did have a boyfriend. His name was Paul, and he was what they call tall, dark, and handsome. I'm guessing he was around six-three or six-four. He was a smooth talker, very charismatic—you know, the type who could sell anything to anyone. The man I told them about was hypermasculine, very athletic, had a chiseled jawline, short black hair with a fade, and smooth, milk-chocolate skin. However, Paul didn't know I was pretending he was my boyfriend.

Paul was a bartender. We met one night in college while he was working. I was at the bar with a friend. After Paul took our food order, my friend and I both looked at one another with our eyebrows raised and a smirk on our face. My friend, who is White, exclaimed, "He's hot, you should go for him." Both of us were single, but I believe in her mind, she was thinking, *Since he's Black, you should go for him.*

Paul certainly was hot; his physique looked like he belonged on the cover of *Men's Health*. I was into him, but I also knew I was attracted to women. But I didn't know if it would be possible for me to even be with a woman, and how would that happen while I was trying to live a heterosexual life? I felt pressured to not be an outlier and just fit in. My friend and I chitchatted at the bar, and I subtly flirted with Paul, showed interest in him, and eventually got his number.

Paul and I started hanging out and spending time together. Within a few weeks, we were taking photos together. "One, two, three, cheese!" I looked down at my phone and saw two pearly white smiles grinning from ear to ear. Snuggling in closely, my arms were wrapped around Paul's waist, my head laid at the top of this chest, with his muscular arm draped over my shoulder. I showed him the photo; he nodded with satisfaction. My friendship with him brought me to meet and get to know other Black men around campus. From what I had noticed, I had never had attention from a man before, let alone many men. Now there was Paul, Quentin, L, Nate, and Elias. They made me swoon, and it was so refreshing to not feel "different" or like an outlier. People saw me for who they saw on the surface. I was expected to date Black men and listen to Motown. I no longer appeared different for being Black, I was expected to *be* Black... only I didn't know how.

Outside of what I learned in school, most of the Black history I knew about was from studying the civil war and learning about Dr. Martin Luther King Jr. I didn't know what soul food was and definitely didn't know how to make it. I had never heard of *Poetic Justice* or *Boyz n the Hood*. I wasn't familiar with Nina Simone or Miles Davis. I had no idea what African American culture and traditions were. On campus, I saw hairstyles I had only previously seen in the movies and clothing styles I surely didn't see at the Gap. And I certainly didn't know how to do my hair. I felt so inadequate and ill-equipped to be the person everyone expected me to be. I was dying on the inside, but I tried, struggled, and grasped to play the part, to be the part, just so I could exist as me.

I thought the best way to understand and learn Black culture was to surround myself with people who were Black. My sophomore year of college, I moved into a townhouse with women I had been friends with since the first week of school, freshman year. Three of the women were from Metro Detroit; two of the women were Black and the third was White. All three were very involved with student life and campus events, and their connections, along with the recent invention of Facebook, helped my racially diverse social circle expand almost overnight. I began to learn about soul food, hip-hop, step dancing, the Kings of Comedy, and cultural norms of millennial African American culture. I got involved with the Black student union and international clubs as I was excited to get to know other Black and African students.

Meanwhile at work, Monday morning coffee and bagel breaks at the law firm always had a similar vibe—"How was your weekend? What did you and your boyfriend do?" my colleagues asked with excited anticipation. I would eagerly share about the weekend adventures Paul and I had together and of course pull up a previous photo from my phone of Paul and me to show everyone. My female colleagues seemed pleased, "He's so handsome." "We're glad you finally found someone." "He looks like a good fit for you." "We can't wait to meet him!" "Are you bringing him to the Christmas party?" I went on sharing about semi-romantic and adventurous stories of Paul, Quentin, L, Nate, and Elias for years. My bosses and colleagues seemed so pleased to think I was finally dating a young, handsome Black man.

I was fearful of coming out of the closet. I felt so pressured to live by everyone's heteronormative standards that I didn't know how to tell anyone I was attracted to women. The more pressure I felt, the more I tried to talk myself into believing I was attracted to those men. After all, it would be easier, right? I thought the more I went through the motions, eventually the motions would turn into feelings and be real. I didn't know how to live as my authentic self without being swept into heteronormative expectations and being the person that society, friends, and colleagues were telling me to be.

---

IT DIDN'T TAKE LONG FOR ME TO SEE homophobia in a lot of the Black people I was near on campus. The Black women I knew often spoke about their desire to be a queen for their man and how to treat their man. I often heard the Black men making "no homo" jokes.

One evening at a female friend's house, when nobody was watching, she and I made out. It was my first kiss with a woman. She was a beautiful Black woman who I knew through mutual

Black men were
disappointed that I didn't
know how to cook soul
food. Black women balked
when I didn't know how
to braid hair.

friends. Our kiss was exhilarating, something I had never experienced before, and I felt the rush throughout my entire body.

My friend told me she didn't have feelings for me because she had a boyfriend. However, nearly every time we saw each other for the next few months, we ended up kissing, and the next day we would always act like it didn't mean anything and that kissing was just for fun. The Black men we hung around seemed to find two women making out attractive, but it was a wrap if emotions or feelings were involved.

My eagerness to fit in and belong as a Black woman eventually diminished into disappointment. Black men were disappointed that I didn't know how to cook soul food. Black women balked when I didn't know how to braid hair. I didn't speak with slang; Black people often told me I sounded White when I spoke and that they were going to take my Black Card. The international African students were disappointed I didn't speak fluent Swahili or French and often told me since I hadn't been back to Africa since I was a kid, I wasn't really African. I wasn't Black enough. I wasn't White enough. I wasn't African enough. The transition from high school to college was much more challenging than I thought it would be. I kept searching for acceptance from others, little by little changing aspects of myself so I could fit in and be the person they wanted me to be.

I no longer had the comfort of football and my close group of loyal friends from high school to rely on. I no longer had the support system I was used to. I heavily relied on my faith being a pillar in my life. My family and I were a part of a small, non-denominational Christian church. My mom became an assistant pastor at our church while I was in high school. I felt a calling to give back as well. While in college, I volunteered with my church as a youth group leader for the high schoolers. Sometimes, at the end of the church service there would be an alter call where you could "give all of your cares to God." Folks would walk up to the stage at the front of the church, express what they needed prayer for, and church leaders would pray for them. I regularly went to the alter call to "pray away the gay." My church believed that homosexuality, among several other things, was a sin. I understood that God doesn't make mistakes, but I didn't understand why He would make me gay if being gay was a sin. At the altar, with tears streaming down my face, I prayed that God would make me straight. The exhaustion of masking behind a role confined by societal, heteronormative, and racial norms was consuming me.

Over the months, which turned into years, alter call after alter call, I prayed to be straight. I confided in one of the youth pastors I was close with and shared how I had been struggling with my identity. What was supposed to have been shared in confidence then turned into rumors that circulated throughout the church and got back to me from a few different people. I was mortified that my trust and confidence had been broken and afraid my family would find out.

I believe Christians have ruined Christianity by allowing self-righteous judgments and hypocrisy to take control, while minimizing the foundational pillars of the Golden Rule and grace and love of God. As the rumors about my sexual orientation circulated, I lost those who I thought were close friends, like dominos, one right after the other. They told me I was a sinner and that I was going to hell—even though I had already accepted Jesus Christ as my Lord and Savior at the age of seven. Most hurtfully, they disassociated themselves with me.

I was wretched and empty. I hated not being straight enough; I hated who I was. After feeling guilty for being in the role, I announced that I needed to take time to focus on college and stepped down from my youth leader position. After other unruly disputes occurred within that church community, most of my family stopped going to that church. Even though I did have some good memories there, I came to realize my faith wasn't the church, or certainly not *that* church. My faith is not my relationship with a building. My faith is my relationship with God.

It was sink or swim, and I felt like I was sinking, and sinking quickly; I played the part—appear "Black," sound "White," be African, act African American, be straight, look Christian. I was absolutely miserable, but this was my new normal. We often play roles to fit in and look or act the part that society wants— the persona works on the outside, but on the inside, we may lack hope, security, and self-acceptance.

In society, whether intentionally or unintentionally, we often project our expectations onto others. I had professors, classmates, bosses, colleagues, and friends expect me to have a Black family because they see I am Black. They didn't see or expect me to be African or adopted or expect me to have a family who is White. Folks I met out and about in the LGBTQ+ community never expected me to be LGBTQ+ because I looked too "femme," even though the term *lipstick lesbian* had been around for decades. It's so important to meet people where they are at, to be present, to show up for them for who they are as an individual, not for simply what we want or anticipate them to be.

When we feel uncomfortable, we are very quick to minimize the identities of others instead of acknowledging those identities and uplifting others and empowering them to live authentically. We should focus on others' strengths, what makes them unique, and what their superpowers are. It takes work, it takes intentionality, and it takes techniques for us to utilize in order to learn how to value others for who they are. Emotional intelligence gives us the ability to have hard or challenging conversations to help us achieve common ground with others, especially if their backgrounds or identities are different from our own. Emotional intelligence allows us to see beyond our own perspectives and better understand, relate to, and communicate with others.

Learning to truly value and respect others for who they are requires the work of putting our ignorance and preconceived notions aside and stepping outside of our own perspectives. It's so crucial that we take the opportunities to understand others, instead of making our own assumptions about their identities. During my time at college and working at the law firm, I strived to embody everything my classmates, peers, bosses, and colleagues expected me to be. I believed if I told them who I really was, or if they found out about my true self, they wouldn't view me as worthy, so I acted the part... I believed the part... I lived the part. My life was an Oscar-worthy role.

———————

WE OFTEN DON'T KNOW when we aren't being true to ourselves, because inauthenticity can surround us and morph into traits that we think are genuine. In order to find out and stay grounded in who you are, check yourself from time to time. How are you showing up? Do you show up in certain environments in a different manner than you do in other environments? Your personality, your style, your clothing, your vernacular, your story... do they reflect the genuine attributes of who you are, or are you presenting yourself a certain way for the approval or expectation of others? What brings you inner peace? I wouldn't have recognized that I was being disingenuous to myself; I was just trying to survive. Being able to come to a place of true inner peace and authenticity, on the contrary to existing in a false sense of security, would have truly made me feel safe, supported, and valued, instead of pretending and playing the Oscar-worthy role.

### FIVE BLACK ICONS I ADMIRE

Growing up, I didn't have many Black people in my life; in fact, there weren't any who I knew very closely. I always looked forward to celebrating Black History Month at school, because it was a time where Black excellence was at the forefront of our daily lives.

**Harriet Tubman** risked her life to help others gain freedom, a life of their own. She inspires me to live a legacy of courage and bravery, helping others find their freedom to live more authentically.

**Dr. Martin Luther King Jr.** taught us that faith and justice go hand in hand. He preached justice, while operating in his faith.

**Emmanuel Acho**'s book *Uncomfortable Conversations with a Black Man* regularly inspires me to try to emulate grace, even with the most ignorant people, during my connections with others in my work and in the world.

**Steve Harvey** gave me hope in bleak times of doubt. I love listening to his motivational speeches on tenacity, faith, and resiliency, when driving toward his purpose.

**Viola Davis** has been breaking glass ceilings her entire career. She leverages her vulnerabilities and turns them into strengths. Also, I love how she continuously uses her platform to empower and celebrate others.

## FIVE WOMEN WHO INSPIRE ME

These five notable women have inspired and impacted me throughout my life.

**Maya Angelou** was a childhood survivor of rape. She didn't speak for nearly five years afterwards. She later exemplified the power of her voice, using it as a catalyst for empowering others.

**Brené Brown**'s book *Daring Greatly* helped save my life, and her book *Braving the Wilderness* helped me see my purpose and power in this world, amidst and because of finding internal belonging even in the eye of adversity.

**Oprah Winfrey**'s vision and ambition inspires me. Even in the most challenging and tumultuous times, she has remained dedicated to her drive and her purpose, using her voice and platform as a force for empowerment.

**Glennon Doyle**'s risk and choice to live authentically empowers me. She breaks societal and heteronormative expectations by being true to herself and honoring love in her same-sex marriage. I'm also empowered by her assertion that "We can do hard things." In times of adversity, this reminds me that we are stronger than we think.

**Shannon Cohen** was the first Black woman in my life who I personally knew who lives a life and career similar to the aspirations I had since college. She has been an example of what is possible.

# 5

# To Live

"People who are hurting don't need Avoiders, Protectors, or Fixers. What we need are patient, loving witnesses. People who sit quietly and hold space for us. People to stand in helpless vigil to our pain."

**GLENNON DOYLE**

I WAS RESPONSIBLE for paying much of my college tuition, therefore I was constantly thinking of ways to make more money. Since I came from a middle-class family, I didn't qualify for financial aid. While working at the law firm, I traded my two-year sales associate role at the Gap for a senior sales associate position at a sister company, Banana Republic, and worked there for almost two years. The new position came with a slight increase in pay and the allure of selling blazers to a more mature clientele instead of selling jeans and hoodies.

At BR, I worked with a clientele similar in background and lifestyle as the colleagues I was working with at the law firm. I understood their language and culture, which was helpful in being successful in the role. The role also came with a 50 percent discount on all clothes, which made it easier to adhere to the law firm dress code. I became fast friends with my new, vibrant coworkers, most of whom were close to my age and quite a few of them were LGBTQ+. Coming into work was always a fun environment where I felt safe and supported. Whenever Lady Gaga's "Just Dance" came on over the sound system, one of my close work friends Dalvin and I would sync into rhythm and start dancing on the sales floor as if we didn't have a care in the world.

With the pressure of wanting to make more money to continue to pay for my college tuition each quarter, I wanted a third job that paid more so I could afford to stay in college.

When I was a young child, my parents would often have parties at our house. My mom loved to host; she was the "hostess with the mostest." When my parents' friends came over, my mom got out the fine china and I played the server, pretending to have a pad of paper in one hand and a pen in the other, taking the guests' drink orders. I remember I loved it! I turned that ambition into a reality by working in the restaurant industry, starting at an Italian restaurant. The income potential with tips, especially at an Italian restaurant where guests were often ordering bottles of wine with their multi-course meals, was much greater than the flat hourly rate selling clothes that Banana Republic could offer. Wanting to keep the discount and loving my role at BR, I was keen on keeping my employment there while finding more hours in the week to have more availability to work. In the interview at the Italian restaurant, the manager, Ramie, saw my strengths and drive even though I didn't have any restaurant experience. I told her I would be one of the best servers she ever had and she believed me.

My part-time job at the law firm became full-time, in the quest to make more money and qualify for health insurance benefits. I changed my college schedule to night classes and was serving at the Italian restaurant on the weekends. My robust schedule called for late-night grocery shopping. One night while I was shopping at a large local twenty-four-hour grocery store, I ran into Dalvin from Banana Republic in the checkouts. He was with a female friend; he introduced us and when I looked into her eyes while shaking her hand, chills overcame my entire body like an electric shock. Everything stood still as I gazed into her big brown eyes. I almost forgot Dalvin was standing there. My height is five-six; she was a couple of inches taller than me, with long, black, wavy hair, her skin silky as milk chocolate, and her smile beaming and bright enough to fill the entire grocery store.

Remembering that Dalvin was there, the three of us exited the grocery store and walked across the parking lot together to our cars. In the parking lot, she and I started sharing our life stories with one another pretty much immediately. In that conversation, we learned we were both adopted, and we both grew up in homogenous areas about ten miles apart from one another. We were both going to college full-time, pursuing the same degree—communications. We both were passionate about people, and we both had weekend jobs working in the restaurant industry. We exchanged phone numbers and at that point, I already knew I needed to have her in my life.

———————

WE SPENT THE NEXT SEVERAL MONTHS being completely inseparable, racing to find a moment, a lunch, a Starbucks date, or a night together just to be in each other's presence, in between our hectic schedules. Our lives became intertwined. In every moment together, the world stood still, replicating the moment we met. She was the only one in the world who made me feel seen, truly seen, as if she was looking into my soul. I fell in love with every part of her. She became my first love, and I became hers.

When we were together, we were fully enjoying being in each other's presence. As our lives became more and more connected, our friend groups merged as well. When we were out in public, friends and strangers regularly commented on how we looked like sisters, our response as we giggled was always, "We're close," often joking with others how we were like sisters.

I was twenty-three years old, and after years of pretending to be in heterosexual relationships, making up fake boyfriends, and years of being single—including middle school and high school relationships—I finally experienced the power of loving and being loved. I had always wanted to be a girlfriend—and to have a girlfriend. It was magical, even though our relationship was our world's greatest secret. Neither of us was out.

We both felt pressured to live for the expectation of our families, our distant friends, our jobs, and society. She came from a very religious Black family and already had a family member who was kicked out of the house for coming out. Her family believed being LGBTQ+ was a sin that would bring you to hell, and they weren't shy about bringing up scare tactics whenever someone mentioned the word *gay*. Only a handful of our close friends knew we were together, but they also knew it was a secret from the rest our worlds and kept the secret safe.

If one of us got out of work before the other, we would often visit each other at work. Sometimes, she would visit me on my lunch hour at the law firm while she was on break in between classes. When my colleagues asked about her, I regularly responded that she was my best friend. Many of my colleagues expected me to be dating a man. I would share stories about the adventures and dates she and I had, but instead of using her name, I would insert random male names, so I could follow suit with my colleagues' expectations of me. She and I were often present at each other's family gatherings, but we told everyone—except for the small group of close friends that truly knew us—that we were best friends.

It was magical, even
though our relationship was
our world's greatest secret.
Neither of us was out.

In our second year together, I had graduated with my bachelor's degree from Grand Valley State University. I had aspired to move to New York City and had ten interviews with Time Warner in Manhattan. We didn't know what the future held for us; she was younger than me, and she was still in school. My graduation in 2009 wasn't the best time for the US economy, after the financial crisis of 2008, to break into a new career without experience. I remained open to staying in Grand Rapids. All we knew was that she and I loved each other and that our love would forever connect us. Even though same-sex marriage wasn't legal then, we would find ourselves dreaming and romanticizing about our wedding.

In chapter 4, I briefly mentioned being run over by a car—my apologies for leaving you hanging. It occurred during this same period when I was searching for a post-college career. What had happened was my grandma and I were walking on a sidewalk, and an SUV driving in reverse on a one-way street drove up the curb and onto the sidewalk, hit me from behind, and continued to drive, running over my body. Thank goodness the distracted driver hit me and not my ninety-something-year-old grandmother. The experience thrust me into the world of insurance claims. Since I had to be on crutches, with my ankle in a cast, frustratingly, the law firm had me go on short-term disability until I no longer needed to be on crutches.

On short-term disability, a talent acquisition specialist from a national insurance company saw me on crutches, and a conversation between us led me to share what happened. The person asked if I had experience with insurance claims. Boy, did I ever! We exchanged contact information and within a week, a career opportunity with that insurance company presented itself. The job duties themselves weren't riveting; however, the salary offer was double what I was making at the law firm, which was more so an indication of how grossly undervalued I was at the law firm, rather than how much I would be making at the insurance company. The human resources and talent acquisition teams of the insurance company saw me as an equal, and right away I felt valued.

Without having the pressure from my law firm colleagues, I decided to no longer pursue law school. I knew the position with the insurance company wouldn't be my dream career, but I recognized it would increase my skillset and be a step in the right direction for me to grow my career and business skills. The increased salary meant that I no longer needed a second job serving nights and weekends. I hung up my black apron and server booklet. I later received a payout from the insurance settlement claim, which enabled me to become debt free.

Have you endured a situation that felt like a series of unfortunate events where doors of opportunities were shutting one right after another? Have you felt like your plans and aspirations were like sand slipping through your fingers? I absolutely know how frustrating and draining that is, especially when we have worked so hard and so long to achieve our goals. Sometimes those are moments that propel us toward the opportunity to evolve in a different direction outside of our realm, which later reveals itself to be the exact journey of a better way through. In the moments during college when I couldn't afford to wipe my butt in my own home, I wouldn't have imagined a freak accident on the sidewalk would lead to six weeks in an ankle cast and a settlement that would change my financial situation.

Being turned down for what was then a dream job in New York City, my favorite city, actually created an opportunity for me to later make an impact in the city I grew up in. We may be experiencing disappointment, loss, or rejection so that we can later discover a silver lining, new possibility, or alternative outcome, allowing us to rise to something greater.

Staying in Grand Rapids meant more time to invest in my relationship. Two years into our relationship, we got matching tattoos to signify that love never fails. We promised each other that even if we ended up hating each other, we would always love our tattoo. Since we were so afraid of being found out or being outed, we never made public displays of affection. I longed to be able to hold her hand or kiss her while walking down the street, but the risk was too great. We enjoyed going to the local gay dance clubs as our only time we could dance closely, flirt, and kiss outside of the four walls of our homes. Nights out at the gay clubs were our escape, unashamed and untamed, a chance to outwardly love like an actual couple.

We also spent a lot of nights in, either just us or with our close friend group. Many of our evenings with friends were filled with dancing in the kitchen—blaring Lady Gaga and Justin Bieber, piling on the couch in the living room for movie nights, or making food together or ordering pizza and laughing and getting the scoop on the latest tea, otherwise known as gossip. The time with our close friends was our safe haven.

One evening we were both at a friend's place, after each of us had a long day and night at work. I was lying in the fetal position, trying to soothe my cramps, and our friend suggested I take ibuprofen. I never took pain meds or medication of any kind, but I was in a world of discomfort, so I gave it a whirl. I took two pills from our friend and ate a Reese's Peanut Butter Cup and a handful of potato chips as the chaser. We ordered takeout and started to watch a movie. About thirty minutes later, my bottom lip started to feel very tight, as if it were being pulled at each end, then my top lip, as if each side of my face were being pulled back in opposite directions. Then my tongue started tingling. I felt my lips with my hand, and they felt hard and hot to the touch. I raced to the bathroom to look in the mirror: my entire face was swollen. In a panic, I called my parents, who told me to go to the ER immediately.

Rushing to the hospital, I felt my throat tightening by the second, becoming more and more difficult to breathe; I had to tip my head upwards just to get a fraction of a breath. I could hardly speak. I didn't know what was going on with my body, and I was panicking. I had never experienced this before. Within twenty-five minutes, I was in the ER, being seen by a doctor, and was hooked up to an IV of epinephrine. Shortly after, my throat felt less tight, and my tongue stopped tingling. The swelling eventually went down. The doctor told me that if I had waited much longer to get the epinephrine into my system, I could have died.

Not knowing if it was the peanut oil from the Reese's Cup or the ibuprofen that caused the reaction, I had a referral to get an allergy test at a specialist the next week. I discovered that it was the ibuprofen that did it. I'm deathly allergic to all NSAIDs, non-steroidal anti-inflammatory drugs, which includes ibuprofen.

———

THE THIRD YEAR OF OUR RELATIONSHIP was a time of change. Our lifestyles and goals were once nearly identical, but we were at a point where our lives and aspirations had moved in vastly different directions. She was younger than me, which didn't feel noticeable until this point. She was into house parties with new bar friends, while I was into networking events with community leaders. We began having a challenging time finding common ground with one another. One evening I went to her restaurant to surprise her at work. The surprise was in fact on me when I arrived. I found her close with a young man she went to school with.

I asked her about him, in front of him, and to my dismay, he responded by saying he was her boyfriend. I told him she and I had been together for three years, and he proceeded to say, "Let's talk about this outside." I was ready to talk to him right then, but I suspected he wanted to talk away from everyone, since we were on the restaurant floor.

He had a medium athletic build and dressed in urban-style clothing, his pants slightly sagging. The three of us went outside to the parking lot of the restaurant. I told him she was my girlfriend, and then he started yelling in my face, saying something along the lines of, "You ain't nothin'! She's been with me for a year."

I was completely dumbfounded and immediately angered. She had mentioned hanging out with him on campus, which I wasn't a fan of and strongly discouraged, because I had a feeling he liked her—she was very likable. They always say your gut is never wrong. My gut told me something was going on with him, but I didn't want to admit it. I had no idea they were spending so much time together, and certainly not for a year. While outside in the parking lot, he became unhinged, punching me and kicking me. I restrained myself from pushing him back, even though I really wanted to.

Instead, I yelled at her, saying, "Really? This is who you want to be with?! Look at him!"

I was on the ground; he was grabbing me, punching my legs as I tried to shuffle away to get out of his grip.

Police pulled into the parking lot; it turned out they were responding to another matter inside the restaurant. They immediately drove up to us, got out of the patrol car, and began separating the three of us.

The police questioned each of us on what had happened. I stated I wanted to file a police report and press charges against him for assaulting me. She said she wanted space from the relationship, and in my shock and heartbreak, I reluctantly honored her wishes.

She and I didn't talk much for the few weeks leading up to the court date. In the investigation, I submitted the photos to the police showing my legs with the bruises from his attack. She was asked by the police to make a statement as the only witness. In her statement, she claimed under oath that I beat myself up because I was jealous of him and upset that she no longer wanted to be with me. The court notified me of her statement, and since the evidence was incongruent with the witness testimony, the charges against him were lowered to a lesser degree of assault.

That was the end of our relationship. She chose to be with him. I wasn't enough for her. I was completely blindsided and anguished.

---

I WENT TO A FEW OF THE FRIENDS who knew about our relationship for support. It turned out they all knew she had been talking to him behind my back and intentionally kept it from me. They supported her decision and stood by her. I was so betrayed—betrayed by her and betrayed by the few friends I had entrusted with my true being. The few people who I opened up to and who saw me for who I was turned their back on me. There wasn't anyone else I could turn to, without coming out, so I just had to live with it destroying me inside like a time bomb.

Meanwhile, I was in a new career, surrounded by strangers. I immediately felt lost and alone in a world of darkness. Once again, I tried to "pray away the gay," but it wasn't working. *Why did God make me like this?* I couldn't be my authentic self with anyone else in my entire life. My world felt like it was over. The devastation and isolation left me withdrawn; I couldn't bare the shame. I couldn't go on; my life was over.

Each day was a smear of numbness, since I believed I couldn't be my authentic self, nor could I see my place or belonging in this world. My desire to no longer live came from a severe disruption in the execution of my purpose. I no longer had a desire to socialize with other friends who didn't know about the situation. I kept to myself and was quiet, and I kept my head down at work.

My trust was broken; my heart was broken; my friendships were broken; my self-esteem was broken. I was broken.

It was the night of Christmas Eve. My plan was to drive my car off the highway overpass. I was driving, nearly in a daze, exceeding one hundred miles per hour, when I abruptly found myself turning the wheel, veering off the highway and over the stark sound of the rumble strip. The sound felt paralyzing to me; I gripped the steering wheel tightly, yet I couldn't bring myself to turn it just a little farther to launch myself off the highway. I continued driving on the outside edge of the lane, eventually centering back into the lane. I couldn't do that because I thought, *What if I hit another car and hurt other people?* I couldn't bear to hurt someone else.

I drove home. It's often noted that people who die by suicide are the ones who are least suspected of suicide. I kept thinking of that, envisioning my funeral with a roomful of acquaintances and distant friends who thought they knew me, having no idea I was living in turmoil.

**FACTS ABOUT SUICIDE**

The Centers for Disease Control and Prevention reports that "Suicide is a leading cause of death in the United States, with 45,979 deaths in 2020. This is about one death every 11 minutes. The number of people who think about or attempt suicide is even higher. In 2020, an estimated 12.2 million American adults seriously thought about suicide, 3.2 million planned a suicide attempt, and 1.2 million attempted suicide."

"Research has shown that people who identify as sexual minorities have higher rates of suicide attempts compared to heterosexual people. Almost a quarter (23.4%) of high school students identifying as lesbian, gay, or bisexual reported attempting suicide in the prior 12 months. This rate is nearly four times higher than the rate reported among heterosexual students (6.4%)."

**Warning Signs of Suicide Contemplation**

According to the National Alliance on Mental Illness, the following are signs someone may be contemplating suicide:

- Increased alcohol and drug use
- Aggressive behavior
- Withdrawal from friends, family, and community
- Impulsive or reckless behavior
- Collecting and saving pills
- Buying a weapon
- Giving away possessions
- Tying up loose ends, like organizing personal papers or paying off debts
- Saying goodbye to friends and family

## SUICIDE PREVENTION AWARENESS RESOURCES

- If you or someone you know is in an emergency, call 911 immediately.

- If you are in crisis or are experiencing suicidal thoughts, call the 988 Suicide & Crisis Lifeline at 988 in the United States or visit 988lifeline.org. They have services in English, Spanish, and for the Deaf and Hard of Hearing.

- If you're uncomfortable talking on the phone, you can also text NAMI to 741741 to be connected to a free, trained crisis counselor on the Crisis Text Line.

- In Canada, you can call Talk Suicide Canada toll free at 1-833-456-4566, or text 45645 between 4:00 p.m. and midnight, or visit talksuicide.ca. According to Talk Suicide, "More than 80% of people who have called Talk Suicide felt an increase in their ability to cope."

- If you identify as LGBTQ+, you can contact The Trevor Project, the world's largest suicide prevention and crisis intervention organization for LGBTQ+ young people, at thetrevorproject.org.

Sadly, on my drive home, I thought of another plan to end my life that seemed to be a less painful route. I knew I had an old bottle of ibuprofen and decided I would take it when I got home. Once there, I proceeded to swallow lots of pills, remembering what happened the last time I took ibuprofen. Sitting on my comfy red couch in my living room, I waited about thirty minutes. Nothing happened. I took more pills and waited... nothing. I look a couple more pills and ended up falling asleep. I woke up to Christmas morning. I was alive. My throat wasn't swollen, my face wasn't swollen, nothing happened; I just fell asleep.

With a combination of being perplexed and confused, I went into my bedroom and grabbed my Bible from a shelf in my closet. I opened up my Bible to read the Christmas story. After all, I felt like it was fitting. I read Luke 2:10, "And the angel said unto them, 'Fear not: for, behold, I bring you good tidings of great joy which shall be to all people.'"

I eagerly continued to the next verse. "'For unto you is born this day in the city of David, a Savior, which is Christ the Lord.'" A peace that I hadn't experienced since I was a young child began to overcome me. I read the passage over and over, "I bring you good tidings of great joy which shall be to all people."

As if the passage descended from heaven, it spoke to my spirit. I was worthy of good tidings of great joy. I was worthy of good tidings of great joy! All people—which includes me. Me, as who I was, as who I was created to be, as who I am, was worthy. I was worthy. I *am* worthy. I am worthy to love, and I am worthy to live.

HOW DO YOU LIVE POST-SUICIDE ATTEMPT? Reach out for help and also practice daily self-care. It's a term we all hear a lot, but what *is* self-care? Self-care is simply doing something for yourself, with the intentional fulfillment of you. Find activities that are enjoyable to you. What brings you joy? What activities make your situation feel less awful? Which activities give you relaxation?

Find activities which are a healthy outlet for your mental health, physical body, and/or spiritual being. In my case, reading the Bible and feeling the peace from God was an outlet that made me realize my worth in this world.

I understand and respect that everyone is coming from different backgrounds. If you are someone who is spiritual, prayer and meditation could be a healthy outlet for you, allowing yourself the ability to disconnect from distractions in our world and refocus on a higher realm including spirituality, our bodies, nature, and the universe.

If you are not spiritual, there are other outlets that could help. Breathing exercises help connect us with our bodies; our focus on our breathing helps slow down our heart rates, especially when we are in a state of panic or anxiety. When our mental state feels all over the place, breathwork can help center us.

Physical movement is another healthy outlet. I recognize that if you are battling with thoughts of loneliness, anxiety, and/or depression, the thought of physical movement may sound exhausting and unobtainable. This is where the power of our minds can raise our emotional feelings. Physical movement in our bodies releases our endorphin hormones. Endorphins give us a natural euphoria, making us feel happy. Endorphins are released through movement which includes cardiovascular activity, exercise, singing, dancing, and creating art.

Physical movement has been vital to my continued mental health. When I found myself in a dark place, I started running. Now let me tell you, I'm not one of those runners who is "a runner." I run like a baby deer with a broken leg, but the key is that I'm moving and have kept with it, literally one step at a time. The important part for me is that movement gives me increased endorphins and gives me more energy than I would have felt had I remained sulking in bed. Endorphins are a natural way to help us cope with stress and pain.

Entertainment can also help increase endorphins and be a healthy outlet. Socializing with others, watching a movie, listening to music, and reading can also help increase endorphins and be a mental escape from your current situations. Sometimes we just need a break for ourselves, and these are ways for our mind to get a break from current stresses.

Finding gratitude is another healthy mental health outlet for self-care. A common phrase people say when we are going through a situation is, "It could always be worse" or "Someone has it worse than you do." While sayings like that may bring slight relief in the moment, it isn't lasting. Basing our level of joy, peace, discomfort, or disappointment in comparison to the situation of others doesn't allow for us to have a solid foundation, nor does it allow for an accurate measurement of the reality for our experience. The way we perceive our experience and how we feel is our reality. Instead of comparing ourselves to others, a healthy exercise is to name the things you are grateful for and focus on what you do have instead of what you don't have or what someone else has or does not have. What you are grateful for isn't something that is fleeting; it is a part of the foundation, part of you. Naming what we are grateful for also speaks to our relationship with others and our relationship within the world around us. Being able to step outside of the things and experiences that bring us down and see how far we have come is powerful. As the saying goes, "We didn't come this far to have only come this far."

Self-care is not selfish. Self-care is crucial. In this place in the world and in the society we are in, with the responsibilities that we have and the pressures we are under, we are being pulled in many different directions. In order for us to pour into others, we need to fill our cups first. If the plane goes down, there is a reason why we need to put our masks on before we put a mask on someone else. We need to take care of ourselves before we can be equipped to help others. If we aren't taking take of ourselves first, we won't have anything left to give. Implementing self-care should be a part of our lifestyles, with continuous regular activity.

It's critical that you also seek help. Find a mental health professional who specializes in the type of turmoil that led to suicidal or destructive thoughts or behaviors. Make sure their beliefs and norms are in alignment with yours. If you can't afford a one-on-one therapist, consider joining a support group, as many are free through community centers and mental health centers.

Don't be afraid to share. Loneliness is a common trait among those who have contemplated or attempted suicide or destruction. We often feel like we are alone and that nobody would understand what we are going through. Share what you are going through with someone who has the capability and capacity to be there for you and help hold you accountable to using healthy coping mechanisms. The person you share with should be someone who is equipped to help you get the adequate supports that are most beneficial to you, should the destructive thoughts or behaviors reoccur. The person has to be someone who is mentally stable and someone who you trust. This can include a therapist, counselor, spiritual leader, mentor, parental figure, or friend. You are not alone.

Consider medication: Sometimes, our body has a chemical imbalance. If you've tried natural and holistic mental health exercises that aren't working for you, consult a doctor you trust for medication options. Be honest with your doctor, as they are there to help you. If money is an issue, speak up about it so they can prescribe a lower-priced medication or direct you to lower-priced pharmacies, or even give you free samples (as some doctors will have these in stock).

———————

AT THE TIME OF MY SUICIDE ATTEMPT, it was 2011, and I was twenty-six years old. Feeling like I didn't have anyone close in my life I could share with and desperately needing support, I called my mom and dad to come over, telling them I had to share something with them. They came over concerned about what I could possibly need to share with them. When they arrived, I couldn't stop shaking. Rocking back and forth, I held my arms across my chest; my anxiety was through the roof.

I knew I couldn't tell them about how I wanted to end my life without telling them about my identity and the breakup and the betrayal, which meant I would be outing myself. Would they accept me? Would they still love me? I had already experienced what felt like rock bottom. I told them I tried to "pray away the gay," and it didn't work and that I didn't want to live.

My mom and dad's response to my coming out to them was angelic. It was everything a child would want to hear from their parents after enduring such intense isolation and agony. They told me they never wanted me to feel like I couldn't share anything with them ever again. They utilized all of the tools someone should use when a loved one shares such information: they listened, they had empathy, they were supportive, they

Would they accept me?
Would they still love me?
I had already experienced
what felt like rock bottom.

weren't judgmental. They just kept saying how much they loved me and how nothing I could do would discontinue their love for me. They told me that I was their daughter and that nothing would change that or their love for me.

My mom and dad's response to my coming out to them gave me immediate relief from all of the pain, shame, and distress I was having with being in conflict with my identity since the age of six. I wasn't ready for the rest of my family, friends, or anyone else in my world to know, but at least I knew I wasn't going to be disowned by my parents. Having that peace was a Christmas gift during that holiday season.

---

WE ARE ALL ON A JOURNEY most others know nothing about. Divine intervention, self-care, and self-love allowed me to realize I am worthy of love, and I am worthy of living. Even when we think we are alone, the reality is, we aren't. I know how scary it can feel to share our journeys with others, especially those close to us, yet the fear and risk of judgment isn't as detrimental as the risk of losing our life. You are not alone.

# 6

# The Interview of a Lifetime

"Your career is what you're paid for. Your calling is what you're made for."

**STEVE HARVEY**

I ENTERED THROUGH the glass double doors of the brown brick building on a warm, sunny morning in June 2013. Through the corridor of the office, I caught a glimpse of one of the employee's computer screens, "TEKsystems Celebrates Pride Month!" I was a bit taken aback in the most refreshing way. I walked across the lobby and asked for the director of operations, Alex Pulido. The receptionist said he would be just a minute and to take a seat. Within minutes the director greeted me and led me to a conference room.

The two of us sat across from each other at the end of the table. I scanned the room to see eight empty black leather swivel chairs surrounding the wooden table and framed aspirational posters on the wall. The director asked me about my education and career history, and I stated I have a bachelor's degree in communications with a focus in public relations and advertising. I then shared that I previously worked at a large law firm for nearly eight years, but my former hopes of being an attorney had been diminished by life's happenstances. I disclosed my feelings of being stagnant and unchallenged in the current role I was in with a large insurance company for nearly two years. I expressed qualities about myself being more driven and self-motivated. I opened up about my interest in opportunities for growth.

The director talked about TEKsystems and their global footprint in the information technology recruiting and services industry. He stated that there were more than a hundred offices across the globe, with room for growth, and that he was hiring self-motivated people to join his recruiting team. He asked me to tell him of a time when I had overcome adversity. The anticipated answer I'm guessing he was expecting was a simple one relating to how or why someone is self-motivated or driven. I'm sure it was a standard interview question the director always asked interviewees.

I immediately thought of being transracially adopted, moving to the United States, and growing up in a homogenous area, and later being a Black female in corporate America, but something about that seemed too easy of an answer. I gave it another thought and answered the question by telling him I was overcoming adversity in that moment by revealing to him that I was gay. The words were spewing out like word vomit. I was twenty-eight years old; I told him I had been keeping my sexual orientation a secret from most of the people in my life, including my family, for more than twenty years. The director listened patiently; his face drew in every word. I shared about being gay and how I felt pressured to live and work as someone I wasn't. The words rolled out so quickly and so naturally, as if I had said them a million times before.

I felt so comfortable with a stranger, potentially my future boss, the director of operations, and then it dawned on me, *I just came out in a job interview!*

Abruptly, the terror began to creep in, and panicked thoughts flooded my head. *Oh my gosh, I just came out in a job interview! Okay, Graci, I'm either going to get this job because of this answer or I'm not going to get this job because of this answer.* I was looking deep into his eyes, wondering if he could feel my sudden angst.

In what felt like the longest pause of eternity, the director's response helped change my life. Alex commended me for being true to myself. He said he never wanted anyone to come to work feeling like they couldn't be themselves or feeling like they had to hide aspects of who they are.

I felt my tense body and upright shoulders ease back, as I slouched into the comfy leather chair. I let out the greatest sigh of relief. For the first time in my professional life, and really in my personal life as well, I knew I was in a safe space where I could finally be my true self. I could be *me*. It was as if a backpack of bricks had been lifted from my shoulders. The rest of the interview questions felt like a breeze, me confidently answering all of the questions asked. Relief and happiness filled my soul for the rest of the interview.

In the next week or so, I received a call from Alex, extending an offer. I proudly accepted the job as an IT recruiter.

————————

BEING SUPPORTED IN AN INCLUSIVE ENVIRONMENT and having the ability to be my authentic self meant I was able to work as my *whole* self every single day. For the first time in my life, I learned to let go of other people's expectations of me. I knew I no longer had to come to work wearing a mask or playing the role of someone I wasn't, or focus my ambitions based on someone else's projections for me. I knew I would be able to be myself at TEKsystems. I could be confident and proud in just being myself. *I was free.*

A few months later, Alex relocated to a different TEKsystems office, and Jon Carpenter stepped in as the new director of operations. Initially, I was worried about no longer having Alex as our director, as his were big shoes to fill. However, fortunately, Jon wore the same size shoes and became the epitome of inclusive leadership. In addition to Jon, my direct boss was Craig Kapuscinski, who saw more potential in me than I had ever seen in myself. He pushed me in the areas I was weak and gave me the courage and confidence to excel in client development, where I was equipped to lead others, including White males who were more than twenty years my senior. Alex, Jon, and Craig invested in me unlike any other leaders I had before. Jon and Craig mentored and sponsored me in business acumen, leadership development, and diversity hiring and retention. They saw my identities as my strengths instead of my limitations.

In Kenji Yoshino's research he states that 50 percent of those who cover in the workplace say it was their leader's expectation of them to cover, which impacted their sense of opportunity and commitment to their work. Prior to working at TEKsystems, I had nearly ten years of corporate work experience, and I was never able to tap into my full potential because I couldn't even walk through the doors as my true self.

Inclusive, equitable environments allow us to be our authentic selves and give us the ability to reach our full potential. If we can't show up as who we are, we are missing out on our purpose and who we are supposed to be.

Have you been in environments where you felt like you couldn't be yourself or you had to minimize parts of who you are just to walk through the door? If so, how did that feel? I know it can be exhausting. Imagine how much more productive we can be in the workplace when we are able to just focus

Inclusive, equitable environments allow us to be our authentic selves and give us the ability to reach our full potential.

on doing our jobs, instead of on covering up identities of who we are. The more inclusive space we are in, the more we're able to embrace our authentic selves, and the less we feel the need to cover at work. We are able to be our best selves when we are able to be our authentic selves. Authenticity happens when we embrace aspects of ourselves and others.

When we aren't able to be our authentic selves, we automatically have barriers around us that limit our trust with others, our communication styles, collaboration tactics, teamwork, and productivity, which directly impacts our contribution to the bottom line. The benefit of prioritizing diversity, equity, and inclusion isn't just because it's the right thing to do or because others are doing it; it also impacts our retention and longevity of profitability. According to Accenture's "Inclusion Starts with I," "Team performance improves by 50% when everyone feels included."

*Diversity* is a term that often gets talked about in media, education, and in the workplace. Diversity is not limited to physical characteristics that we see on the surface like gender, age, and race. There is so much more to diversity than the physical attributes we can see. Diversity is everything that encompasses us; in addition to the physical traits it also includes our diversity of thought, diversity of experience, diversity of background, diversity of perspectives, diversity of talent, diversity of skill. Diversity is everything we bring to the table.

*Inclusion* is ensuring we are included, with a seat at the table and a voice at the table. Inclusion is ensuring we are being seen, being heard, and being valued for everything we have to offer. We build inclusion by valuing people for the identities they are, the backgrounds they have, and the journeys they've lived. If our environment doesn't have inclusion, then our diversity doesn't matter.

I eagerly came to work and came ready to work, every single day. Each morning, I cheerfully greeted everyone on my way to my desk. I was no longer fearful of being "found out." I was proudly showing my true colors. I was able to open up to my colleagues and build strong, genuine relationships with them. Having a solid foundation of mutual respect and trust increased our collaboration, teamwork, and productivity. The colleagues I worked alongside became some of my closest friends. They supported me by taking time to understand my background, my passions, my goals, and my interests, while congruently valuing other perspectives outside of themselves, to meet me where I was at. I had never felt so safe and seen in a workplace.

TEKsystems was a company that leveraged equity as a part of their diversity and inclusion strategy. Equity and equality are often incorrectly believed to be synonymous with one another. *Equality* is providing the same tools to everyone; equality means fairness, equal treatment for all. *Equity* also means equal outcomes or opportunities for all. But equity is providing the right tools for those who need them in order for everyone to have equal opportunities and equal outcomes. If three people of different heights are all trying to reach something on the top shelf, the tallest person may be able to reach it on their own without any assistance. The shortest person may need to stand on the second rung of a ladder to reach the top shelf. The person with the middle height may only need to stand on the first rung of the ladder to reach the top shelf. Equity is providing the opportunity of having a ladder with rungs so that all three people with different dimensions of diversity can receive and achieve the same outcome.

TEKsystems was a company that didn't just preach about the importance of diversity, equity, and inclusion, they lived it. I joined and co-led TEKsystems' multicultural, women's, and pride employee resource groups (ERGs), which were employee-led, affinity-based groups with a purpose of building empowerment, creating belonging internally and externally, and connecting with clients and community. My colleagues taught me what allyship was: half of the office was involved with the ERGs, including leaders Jon and Craig. My colleagues were true allies who were present, who listened, who were willing to risk their privilege and meet me where I was at.

Most of my straight, cisgender colleagues knew I was a newly out queer. *Queer* is often used as an all-encompassing umbrella term for LGBTQ+. For me, queer, or the *Q* in LGBTQ+ means I'm not straight. I'm not saying I'd never be with a man; however, I know I prefer women. In the past, the word *queer* was often used as a pejorative, but it has since been positively reclaimed by many members of the LGBTQ+ community.

Prior to me working at TEKsystems, many of my colleagues had never been to a pride parade before, yet within a couple of years our office became a major sponsor, volunteering at all of the main LGBTQ+ events in our city. I had leaders who showed empathy and vulnerability, and they were willing to grow and learn in the areas they weren't as versed in. It wasn't the queer people in gay bars, coffee shops, or within the community who initially helped make me feel supported and accepted. It was my straight, cisgender colleagues. They valued me for who I was and weren't afraid to use their voices or platforms to help empower all aspects of my identity.

---

TEKSYSTEMS PROMOTED EMPLOYEE WELL-BEING and personal growth through leadership development programs, the ERGs, and self-help and inspirational readings recommended by the executive leadership. Working as my authentic self gave me the opportunity to work toward my potential. I was quickly excelling. My increase in performance and income drove me to invest more in my personal development. A TEKsystems DEI executive and mentor, Michelle, recommended me the works of inspirational author Brené Brown. From what other leaders shared with me, I knew investing in my personal growth would have a direct effect on my continued increase of performance and positioning in the company.

I was deeply drawn to Brené Brown's work. She explains simple everyday concepts of shame, courage, and vulnerability in the most profound ways. Her words spoke directly to my soul, and her concepts helped me work through the shame and guilt I had been holding on to. I also learned that my vulnerability was a strength. Through reading Brown's book *Braving the Wilderness*, I learned to address many of the shame-related inequities I was holding on to. I saw the things that made me feel shameful and harnessed that energy into vulnerability and courage, which increased the authenticity in friendships and work relationships.

I've since become much more social by expanding my friend group with people who were more aligned with my values, and I've also become involved in the local Grand Rapids LGBTQ+ community, volunteering on local LGBTQ+ boards and committees. I learned how to be a support, resource, and ally for others in the way others had shown up to support me.

One of my favorite Brené Brown quotes (I have so many favorites) is from *Braving the Wilderness*. She states, "People are hard to hate close up. Move in."

Being uncomfortable with the unfamiliar is human nature. When we are introduced to a new person, a new concept, a new idea, a new lifestyle that is unfamiliar to us, our instinct is to be

We need to get
into the habit of being
comfortable with being
uncomfortable.

uncomfortable with it, but we need to get into the habit of being comfortable with being uncomfortable. Growth comes from discomfort. I know growing pains don't feel good, but when we have growing pains, we are able to gain more and become stronger. Don't put yourself in harm's way or in a dangerous situation. While in a physically safe environment, when we learn to take one step toward our discomfort, we are able to grow in new areas, and when we grow, there is probably someone on the other end of that equation who receives the opportunity to grow as well.

I know it can sometimes feel awkward to engage with someone who may look different from us, or have a different background than us, or someone with a different lifestyle or religion than us. However, when we step outside of our comfort zones and learn to put our stigmas and biases down and value the person for who they are, we will likely discover we have more in common than we realized. You might be thinking, *I don't know where to begin... I don't know what to say to someone different from me... I don't want to say the wrong thing.*

In the words of Maya Angelou, "I've learned that people will forget what you said, people will forget what you did, but people will never forget how you made them feel." What matters the most is where your heart is and what your intentions are. And guess what? We are human; we might say the wrong thing, we might mess up... and that's okay. We can't let the fear of making a mistake prevent us from engaging with others. If you mess up, be authentic and own it.

Not long ago, I made a mistake and misgendered a friend of mine, referring to them by the incorrect pronoun. I was in my friend's presence when it happened. I immediately took responsibility and apologized to my friend and the others I was talking to, and then repeated the sentence, using the correct pronoun. When we make a mistake, we don't have to create a grandiose gesture, simply acknowledge, take responsibility, and move forward by correcting your mistake.

Inclusive leadership and allyship is like a toolbox; it's not very useful if we just walk around carrying it like a badge. It becomes beneficial when we take out the tools and go to work. As a society, we have grown accustomed to believing allyship is simply changing our profile photo and running in a 5K race for wounded warriors or autism. We think that putting up a rainbow flag in June or wearing pink in October means that we are allies, but that's like walking around with a locked toolbox, saying you work in construction. Being an ally means we need to access our tools and put them to work for others.

Equitable environments are spaces where leaders, colleagues, students, neighbors, friends, families, and others are grounded in their allyship by utilizing their tools. These tools include being present; listening; speaking up; using their voices or platforms for others with less access or privilege; publicly advocating for equality and equity; confronting bias, discrimination, or harassment; volunteering their time; donating funds or items of value; emotionally or spiritually supporting, mentoring, or sponsoring based on a cause or community with less privilege or access. Changing profile photos and running in 5K races for a cause or a cure are great, but that cannot be all we are doing when we say we are an ally. Being an ally or an inclusive leader is an equitable action that takes work: it means effectively leading and showing up for others even when their backgrounds or experiences are different from our own.

We often devalue the power of our voice as an equitable tool. We may think, *Well, I'm just one person.* Your voice is powerful. In case you missed it, I'll say it again for the people in the back, your voice is powerful! If you see an injustice happening, say something. Sometimes, all it takes is one person to speak up, one person to say, "That's not cool," "We don't use that language here," "That's not funny," "That's not true," "Don't say that," "That's not appropriate." All it takes is one person to speak up to create an impact. We're used to being quick to say something in order to prevent someone from being in physical danger: "Caution: wet floor." "Don't slip on that." "Be careful." "This is hot." "Watch out." The same principle should apply for our emotional safety. If you see something, say something.

Many of us have some privileges, more or less than others of us. Privilege doesn't mean you've lived a privileged life because of your identity. Privilege doesn't mean you haven't had to work hard for what you have. Privilege doesn't mean you didn't have to rise up and pick yourself up from your bootstraps. Privilege simply means *access*. When we have access, we have opportunity. Having privilege means certain aspects of your identity do not present themselves as limits or barriers to access. We can have more privilege or less privilege based on our race, ethnicity, gender expression, sexual orientation, age, ability, religion, familial status, career status, socioeconomic status, education, geographical location, or other aspects of our identity. When we have privilege, we have an opportunity to use it as a tool for empowerment. When we leverage our privilege for the empowerment of others, we become an ally.

Inclusive leaders leverage their privilege to help provide or advocate for access in order for everyone to have equitable outcomes. Inclusive leadership and allyship in the workplace help increase employee engagement and retention by elevating employee experience. Inclusive leadership helps increase forward mobility and opportunity for advancement. In client meetings, Craig leveraged his privilege for my benefit by intentionally having me lead the meetings with many of our clients.

Me, a Black millennial female, leading meetings with clients who were White males, one to two decades older than me. This helped set a precedent of power and gave me confidence and competence in my work, while also breaking down biases or preconceived notions the clients could have of me. Craig's confidence in me allowed my clients to have confidence in me, too.

Jon used his privilege, his tenure in the company, and his access to senior leadership to sponsor me and advocate for me to be a part of a corporate leadership development program for high-potential employees. Jon's access and belief in my potential positioned me to be in meetings and networking circles with the most senior leaders of TEKsystems, including the president of the company. Jon knew my skillset, diverse background, and perspectives would be a value-add to the organization. Jon advocated for opportunities for me to work on special projects that gave me more exposure at a corporate level than the local office could provide.

According to a 2021 study by McKinsey & Company and Lean In, in the United States, women of color currently comprise only 4 percent of C-suite positions, in comparison to 20 percent White women, 13 percent men of color, and 62 percent White men. The stark 4 percent isn't due to lack of talent and ability; it's largely due to lack of access—lack of access to opportunity, lack of access to decision-makers, lack of access to development programs, mentorship, and sponsorship, etc. Being a part of the leadership program at TEKsystems gave me access—privilege— to networks and the opportunity to learn from other leaders in the company who had roles, like diversity and inclusion positions, that were aspirational to me in my career goals.

Inclusive environments allow us to be our authentic selves and bring our whole selves to work. The same inclusive leadership approach can be applied to education, community

**"**

Privilege simply means *access.* When we have access, we have opportunity.

**"**

engagement, and within our personal lives. Working in the equitable environment of TEKsystems, under Jon and Craig's inclusive leadership, gave me the opportunity to soar toward my potential and positioned me to work in the field of diversity, equity, and inclusion, which changed and enhanced the trajectory of my life.

---

WHEN WE START SEEING OURSELVES as a dimension of diversity, then we can see ourselves as part of the solution of inclusion. We aren't going to boil the ocean today, but we can create a ripple effect and begin creating an impact in the world around us today. What is one action step you are committed to doing to be an ally, an inclusive leader, or to increase equity and inclusion in your world?

The work of diversity, equity, and inclusion is just that, work. It takes work and intention to embrace diversity, implement equity, and increase inclusion in an environment.

**TEN WAYS TO EMBRACE DIVERSITY AND INCREASE INCLUSION IN YOUR WORKPLACE**

1 **Ensure the leadership team and/or board is reflective of the communities you serve.**
Having adequate representation helps better serve your clients and communities by delivering service from their perspectives.

2 **Hire from a diverse candidate pool.**
Make an effort to accept candidates from different backgrounds. This will help make your organization more diverse.

3 **Become involved with community organizations.**
This helps bring fresh ideas and innovation into the workplace while creating employee volunteer opportunities.

4 **Build relationships with underrepresented community organizations.**
This helps build your networks with hiring pools and corporate social responsibility.

5 **Create employee resource groups, networks, or affinity groups.**
This helps build a sense of belonging within the organization in addition to providing relationship-building and networking opportunities.

6 **Incorporate mental health days.**
More than one in every four adults in the United States experience a mental health issue per year. Having mental health days helps ensure that employees are empowered to prioritize their mental health.

7   **Add mental health into wellness health benefits.**
Prioritizing employees' mental health enables your people to have the resources to put their best foot forward.

8   **Invest in underrepresented groups.**
Put your money and actions where your mouth is. Actions speak louder than words.

9   **Create policies that support equitable outcomes for all.**
Policies help ensure the longevity of an equitable and inclusive work environment.

10  **Incorporate flexible work-life balance.**
Working during and through the pandemic shows we have innovated new ways of working with equal or increased rates of productivity, while minimizing burnout.

# 7

# To Love

"And love is love is love is love is love is love is love is love cannot be killed or swept aside… Now fill the world with music, love and pride."

LIN-MANUEL MIRANDA

I WAS TWENTY-EIGHT years old, keen on building my professional circles and networking within the community. I was involved in several community-based organizations and was seeking to expand my impact within the city, particularly within the Black, Brown, and LGBTQ+ communities, since I was newly out and proud. I met K at a lesbian networking event. We hit it off right away. She was the first person I was interested in since my heartbreak. Through faith, time, self-care, and self-love, I had learned and knew my value in life and my value in love.

K was unlike other women I had crushed on. We were in very different places in life, and she had a teenage son from a previous marriage. I think the allure of something new, from both of our perspectives, brought us together. Our relationship started off strong and became serious very quickly. In stereotypical lesbian fashion, within only a few months of dating, we rented a U-Haul and moved in together. We were very eager to be a family. Remembering what my parents had shared with me two years prior, when they accepted me after I confided in them about my previous relationship, instead of keeping this relationship a secret, this time I was eager to tell them.

I excitedly went to my parents' house to tell them the news of being in a relationship with K. When I shared the news, to my dismay, they responded drastically differently from when I came out to them a couple years ago. As someone who always tried to please my parents and be an overachiever, a very common trait of adoptees, my dad's response that he was disappointed in me struck like a dagger into my soul. Shockingly, my parents also said they didn't want me to share my relationship on social media, as they didn't want others in our family and their social circles to know. The shock of their reaction and their shame toward me was almost paralyzing. How could these be the same people—my mom and dad—who were there for me in my darkest moment, now be disappointed in me... for finding love again and being happy?

My parents stated that they were fearful my life would be harder than it already was, as they had witnessed the challenges I had faced as a Black African immigrant. I believe, in addition to their shame and their religious beliefs, they were also worried I wouldn't do as well at work and wouldn't be as successful as straight White counterparts. My mom and dad said they thought when I came out to them before that I was going through a phase and since I didn't date another woman for two years after, they somehow thought I was no longer attracted to women. I believe they thought being LGBTQ+ would be one more thing that could cause discrimination or rejection, not realizing that *they* were the ones who were being discriminatory and non-accepting.

I then called all of my siblings, nieces, and nephew individually to come out to them. After my parents' reaction, I didn't want them to be the ones to tell the rest of my family, and I believed my family deserved to hear it from me directly. Because of the large age difference between my siblings and me,

**"**

The truth is that the experience of coming out more often consists of more circular moments, rather than milestone achievements.

**"**

half of my nieces and nephew were close to my age, and the others didn't trail far behind. All of my nieces and my nephew were loving and accepting toward me when I came out to them. They responded as if it was no big deal. Most of my siblings, not all, but most, had a much different reaction. It can feel so liberating to come out to ourselves, but it can feel so debilitating to come out to others who don't understand or agree with our identities.

My relationship with my family took a severe hit after coming out for the second time. As a society, we often think of "coming out" as a one-time thing. The truth is that the experience of coming out more often consists of more circular moments, rather than milestone achievements. Many in the LGBTQ+ community are constantly coming out, over and over. Every time we show up to new spaces and meet new faces, when we talk about our personal lives, introduce a significant other, fill out workplace benefits information, there is often the pressure of coming out, again and again. I imagine my family and I were both in mourning. I was mourning not having them as close in my life and mourned the shame and disappointment they extended toward me. They were mourning the loss of their expectations of me and what they projected my future to be.

The Kübler-Ross Grief Cycle brings us through the five stages of grief: denial, anger, bargaining, depression, and acceptance. In my eyes, it appeared my parents' grief began when I told them about my new relationship with K, but in reality, it more than likely began when I came out to them the first time, two years prior. They said all of the right things on the surface, which kept me alive, but were probably internally living in denial.

When I brought my sexual orientation up again with a new relationship, their anger kicked in, and my mom and dad and most of the rest of my family went through the grieving process. As humans, we put so much pressure and value on our expectations of other people. We often get hurt when our expectations aren't met. My parents had high expectations of me, as I had high expectations of them, which resulted in all of us being shattered.

———————

WORK WAS MY SAFE SPACE. Being able to show up authentically at work, and having leaders who accepted all parts of me, allowed me to submerge myself into my work without limitations. I was bound and determined to be successful, not despite of my identities, but because of them. The intersectionality of my identities allowed to me develop deeper, meaningful connections with my colleagues, clients, and community, which in turn helped all of my colleagues work more authentically, more collaboratively, and more productively. In the back of my mind, or perhaps it was in the forefront of my mind, I also wanted to prove to my family, and the rest of society, that I could be LGBTQ+ and Black and successful, all at the same time. I wanted to prove it to the world. I didn't have Black LGBTQ+ leaders in my life who were role models for me. I was determined to be that leader for others, to make representation a reality in the workplace. We aspire to be what we can see.

Throughout our lives, we are going to have loved ones disappointed in us, and we will be disappointed in our loved ones. People we know, and those we don't, will say things either intentionally or unintentionally that may crush or betray us. During those difficult moments, stay in tune with your mental health and establish healthy boundaries to protect yourself. Your energy is sacred; don't use it on people or things who don't deserve it.

For those who do deserve your energy in having crucial conversations, communicate in a safe, neutral space. Take a deep breath, or many deep breaths, to lower your heart rate. Openly listen to hear what the other person has to say, not to listen to respond. Our families, for instance, and people we love and respect, deserve our understanding. Even though some members of my family and I didn't agree with one another, we deserved to be heard and understood. If you don't understand a loved one or if you have questions, seek to understand in an empathetic and non-judgmental manner. We aren't always going to agree with others, and they aren't always going to agree with us, but we all deserve to be respected and heard. Acknowledge the situation and that you've understood what the other person is communicating.

If you still don't understand, continue to seek to understand by asking non-defensive, open-ended questions such as, "What do you mean by that?" "What is this based on?" "Where is this coming from?" "Tell me more about that." "Can you share with me why this matters to you?" "What does this mean to you?" "How are you feeling after communicating this?" Asking open-ended questions like these are productive ways to continue to learn from one another in conversation.

After both parties have shared their thoughts, understood, and acknowledged the situation, you need to establish next steps. What would you like from the other person? How would you like the relationship to continue? How would you like to move forward? At the end of the conversation, we still may not agree with one another; however, we will have given what the other deserves, to be heard and to be understood, which allows for a more authentic and genuine connection between the two parties. These are communication techniques you can use, whether it's for conversations with coworkers, friends, or loved ones—and having a plan for the language you use can especially help when you are emotional or heated in the moment.

I also wanted to prove to
my family, and the rest of society, that
I could be LGBTQ+ and Black and
successful, all at the same time.

So many of us have been labeled, boxed in, or defined by others. Let *you* define you. It's important for us to be true to ourselves and live our truths, even when it hurts, as long as we aren't harming others or ourselves. We can't control other people's reactions when they don't understand or agree with our identities; we can only control our actions. As much as I wish I could have controlled my family's reaction, it wasn't my responsibility. They had to live their own journeys. Just like grieving, growth is a process. As they were on their journeys, I was on my own journey of learning to find belonging from within, instead of from others. I was made the way I was for a reason. For years, I thought I wasn't enough based on other people's expectations. I learned I am more than enough because I'm one of His creations.

---

AFTER A FEW MONTHS OF A TURBULENT RELATIONSHIP with my family, my mom sent an email to all of us, inviting everyone over for a family BBQ dinner. Throughout various times in my life, my parents would regularly host family dinners. In the body of the email, my mom said she was making ribs and asked my siblings to bring a side dish or dessert. She asked who was coming over so that she had a headcount. The email chain responses included the list of dishes and suggestions for what each sibling should bring. The chain concluded with my mom stating, "Graci, feel free to bring K and her son."

*This must be a typo*, I thought. Bewildered, I read the emails over and over and then called my mom to ask her about K and her son being there. She stated, "If I'm going to claim to be a true Christian, then I need to love and accept you and whomever will be in your life."

After my mom and dad accepted my identity and relationship, the rest of my family began a process of outwardly accepting me for who I am, instead of who they wished I was. On the one hand, man-made religious fundamentals were a driving factor of the dissolution between my family and me, yet on the other hand, faith and grace are also what brought us back together. I believe in a God who believes in love. I believe in a God who is love. Sometimes, the process of coming out can take some time for others. Truthfully, we may not want to give others the grace or patience it can sometimes take, and I know how hard that is. I also know that meeting others where they are and having grace and patience for them on their journey can be very beneficial in healing, learning, and growth.

––––––––––––

COMING OUT IS A JOURNEY. I understand the pressure we can feel to come out. Don't feel pressured by someone else's timeline. Do what is right for you and on your own time. Sometimes, our environment isn't conducive to or accepting of our LGBTQ+ selves. If you're able, align yourself with people you trust, allies and environments that support your whole self, so you don't have to feel alone. Don't forget to prioritize your mental health during the coming out process. And if you don't feel comfortable coming out, that is okay. For those of you who have been shamed into thinking you aren't worthy, I know that hurt and I have lived that rejection. Don't let anyone try to dim your light. You are fire. The world needs the light you radiate. You are a force. You are enough. You are more than enough. There is no one else like you, and the world is better for it. Your life is worth living. You are worthy of life and you are worthy of love.

## BOOKS AND RESOURCES FOR THOSE COMING OUT

### PFLAG

Founded in 1973, PFLAG is the first and largest organization dedicated to supporting, educating, and advocating for LGBTQ+ people and their families. This is a good starting place if you need support: pflag.org.

### Books for Your Own Shelf

- *LGBTQ: The Survival Guide for Lesbian, Gay, Bisexual, Transgender, and Questioning Teens* by Kelly Huegel Madrone

- *It Gets Better: Coming Out, Overcoming Bullying, and Creating a Life Worth Living* edited by Dan Savage and Terry Miller

- *Sister Outsider: Essays and Speeches* by Audre Lorde

- *Fun Home: A Family Tragicomic* by Alison Bechdel

- *Boy Erased: A Memoir of Identity, Faith, and Family* by Garrard Conley

- *No Ashes in the Fire: Coming of Age Black & Free in America* by Darnell Moore

- *Here for It: Or, How to Save Your Soul in America: Essays* by R. Eric Thomas

- *Untamed* by Glennon Doyle

**Books for Families Seeking Gender Support**

- *A Quick & Easy Guide to They/Them Pronouns by* Archie Bongiovanni and Tristan Jimerson

- *Being You: A First Conversation about Gender* by Megan Madison and Jessica Ralli, illustrated by Anne/Andy Passchier

- *Love Lives Here: A Story of Thriving in a Transgender Family* by Amanda Jetté Knox

- *The Gender Creative Child: Pathways for Nurturing and Supporting Children Who Live Outside Gender Boxes* by Diane Ehrensaft

## 8

# My Child.
# My Child.
# My Child.

"We all reach a point as young adults when we wonder what we should be doing with our lives—or, at the very least, which direction to point ourselves in. Beyond the means to get by, we need to think about what's most important to us. Not surprisingly, I discovered that for me the answer was family."

**SAROO BRIERLEY**

"TGIF!" I EXCLAIMED as I raised my glass for a toast and took a sip of my Ketel One vodka and cranberry juice. Ketel One vodka is my go-to vodka, in honor of my dad's Dutch heritage. And cranberry juice, because it's good for your health, right? It was 2015, I was twenty-nine years old, kicking off a winter weekend with cocktails, appetizers, and socializing with old and new friends at one of my favorite local sports bars, Peppino's, on that brisk January night. K and I had broken up the previous year, but we remain friends to this day. Single and ready to mingle, I scanned the circle of friends, creating small talk about the work week, when I came across one person in the group whom I hadn't met yet. Being polite and rather social, I introduced myself to her—her name was Kate. In our initial greeting, she asked, "Where are you from?"

Being asked that question on a regular basis, naturally, I replied, "I've lived in Grand Rapids most of my life, but I'm originally from the Congo."

I'm not sure if I'm regularly asked the question because some people think I have an accent, or if I'm asked the question because my vernacular doesn't always align with what some expect an African American would sound like. By saving people the confusion and saving me the awkwardness, I just tell them fully where I'm from.

I was pleasantly surprised and intrigued by Kate's response, "Which Congo? The Republic of the Congo or the Democratic Republic of the Congo?"

Kate and I quickly became engaged in conversation as we chatted about her knowledge of Africa. Kate was a middle school social studies teacher who during that time was teaching her seventh graders a unit on Africa. I was impressed with her knowledge of African cultures and history, and I shared with her about my birth and my adoption. As I spoke, her face lit up and she burst with excitement, "I'm teaching my classes about the Rwandan Genocide next week! You have to share your story with my classes!"

Kate wanted me to talk about my experience living in the Congo and share with the students what the American Dream means from the perspective of an immigrant. I was taken aback and immediately felt intimidated to think my story would somehow be relevant to the Rwandan Genocide and connected to the American Dream, with a room full of twelve- and thirteen-year-olds. Doubts flooded my head as I felt ill-equipped. I told her I was nearly four when we moved to the United States. As a child, I had no concept of the bordering country Rwanda nor knowledge of the civil unrest, which turned into war.

As I looked down at my cocktail, I pondered whose childhood story I could share with Kate's students. While I pondered, it dawned on me, there was someone I knew whose story I might be able to share with the students—Hannah from the orphanage. Hannah was the daughter of the orphanage missionaries who had the toy doll bassinet I was lying in when my mom found me. Hannah was about seven years older than me, and I thought she may have memory of those times. Hannah kept in touch with my siblings, since they were closer to her age than I was, and Facebook had kept them in contact over the years. Even though I didn't have recollection of knowing Hannah while living in Congo, we were connected on Facebook, and she was then living in Kenya. The evening at Peppino's concluded with me telling Kate that I was going to reach out to Hannah and ask her if I could share her story for the potential presentation.

A couple of days later, I reached out to Hannah through Facebook Messenger to ask her about her childhood during the Rwandan Genocide. Hannah seemed delighted to hear from me. She stated her family, the Smiths, were safe during the time of the Rwandan Genocide. I asked her what she did during that time from the moment she woke up to the moment she went to bed. She wrote that her family would wake up in the morning and pick crops and hike into the mountains to bring MariJani food.

I was perplexed and confused to find out Hannah even knew my biological mother. As far as I knew, MariJani was struggling with every breath to stay alive as she gave birth to me. My entire life, I thought my biological mother was dead. From time to time, I would think of her—I would wonder what it would be like to look like someone and have similar mannerisms as someone.

Hannah continued to tell me her family took care of Mari-Jani after my family moved to the United States.

Not knowing anything about MariJani, I nervously yearned to learn *something* about her, so I cautiously asked Hannah what MariJani was like. Hannah eagerly replied, "She was sweet. She smiled a lot and loved people."

Tears slowly streamed down my face as I began to imagine her as part of me. In my adult life, I have been told my smile lights the room, and I'm also very passionate about people—the

My entire life,
I thought my
biological mother
was dead.

first traits we had in common. I wondered, was that nature or nurture—where did that come from?

Every message I received from Hannah, I read over and over, almost as if her knowledge of MariJani was too much to handle and also too scary and too exciting to not know more.

———

I TOLD KATE I WOULD BE ABLE TO SHARE Hannah's story with her students and conveyed the shock that Hannah knew my biological mother, MariJani. Kate eagerly asked me if I knew if MariJani was still alive. Painfully, I explained I thought she was dead, but I didn't know when she died. Kate didn't understand how I didn't know exactly, and she urged me to ask Hannah to find out.

Sometimes, we don't want to ask the question we are too afraid to know the answer to. This was one of those times. I was too scared to get the answer and didn't know how I would handle it, whatever the answer may be. I had a sense of comfort with the unknown. Ignorance is bliss. The unknown meant I didn't have to confront reality, but the truth kept nagging at me. I tried to stuff it away, I tried to put it in the back of my head, but somehow the desire to confront the truth kept rising to the forefront. For the next forty-eight hours, the desire to know tugged stronger and stronger to the point where I could no longer ignore it—out of affliction, I mustered up the courage to ask Hannah if MariJani was still alive. I knew that whatever the answer was would be challenging to process, but at least I would have peace of mind knowing that I did what I could to find out.

Hannah quickly replied to the message by saying she didn't know but thought she may have died twenty years prior, although she would ask around to find out. As my heart raced, my curiosity continued to grow. I needed to know. I needed to have closure of knowing when she died. I begged Hannah to ask anyone she could and find out any information she was able to about MariJani. I desperately needed a time frame, a date, something... anything.

A few nights later, I was asleep on the couch; my phone was tucked underneath me. At 1:15 a.m., I was startled as I woke from the vibration of my phone. I was baffled at who would be contacting me so late. As my eyes adjusted to the phone, through the blur, I read it was a notification from Hannah. I jolted up on the arm of the couch. I could feel my heart beating out of my chest, both eyebrows raised, my eyes opened widely as I opened the message.

In Hannah's message, she was referring to a conversation she was having with her friend who lives in the Congo. Hannah asked her friend if MariJani is still alive. The friend replied, "Yep, she is still alive. Two weeks ago, she came after me in Kidodobo, asking about her daughter, but I did not have a clue." I read the message over and over in disbelief as if I was expecting the words to change. I read it again, I couldn't believe it—the daughter Hannah's friend was referring to was *me*!

Hannah's friend didn't have a clue about who I was, since I was adopted so young. Tears filled my eyes and quickly plummeted down my face. I read the message over and over again, then another message came in, stating I have two younger biological brothers from a different father, and that the boys' father had passed away. More disbelief—I almost couldn't believe what I was reading. I was immediately overwhelmed and overcome with joy and confusion. Questions about Mari-Jani flooded my head: *What is she like? How is she still alive? Do my parents know she isn't dead? How old is she? What does she look like? Does she know that I am alive?*

Then I was sobbing uncontrollably. I sobbed for the rest of the night and continued sobbing as I woke up.

———————

IN THE MORNING, I CALLED KATE to tell her the news. She was ecstatic, but I was still in shock. I told her I had to inform my mom and dad but was intimidated and afraid of how they would react. I was even more nervous to tell them MariJani was alive than I was when I came out to them. Kate offered to come with me to my parents' house on that Sunday.

When we arrived at my parents' house, my heavy breathing became an excessive panting. I kept clenching my fists together and opening them back up and clenching again. Kate and I sat across from my mom and dad in the living room. My parents had never met Kate before. I'm sure they were equally as nervous and wondering why I was acting so fearful. The thoughts that were running through my head were: *Is telling them betraying them? Will they be upset? Will my desire to meet my biological mother take away from my love of my mom and dad?* The last time I told my mom and dad big news, it didn't go well at all; I felt hesitant to tell them anything else newsworthy, out of fear of their reaction.

Looking down at my clamped hands and then back up at my mom and dad, I somehow blurted out the words, "MariJani is still alive."

Their reaction was silence... complete shock; they looked straight at me with blank stares... then more silence. I didn't understand why they were so silent or what they were thinking.

Their silence felt like it lasted an eternity. My dad, normally pensive, following wise words, had nothing to say. My mom, outgoing and demonstrative, remained silent. I broke the silence by telling them I needed to meet her and that I needed them to come with me. I needed to say thank you to MariJani; her giving me up gave me life. I also needed my mom and dad to be there so MariJani could see how much they love me and the opportunities I have been given.

I couldn't tell if I was shedding happy tears or sad tears—perhaps it was a combination of both—nonetheless, both of my parents agreed to start planning the trip to the Congo. My mom said they didn't know how we could get into the Congo and how we would find MariJani, but she believed and had faith God would provide a way. I had faith as well. I couldn't find out she was alive and then not have the ability to meet her. MariJani was still living in a mud hut, without internet or phone access. I didn't have a way to communicate with MariJani to tell her I was coming to meet her, nor did she know that I knew she was alive and asking about me. She had no idea we were planning to meet her. I had no clue how she would feel about meeting me, or if she even wanted to meet me.

Over the next few days, my emotions flooded, and my mind continued to race: *Do I look like her? Will she be proud of me? Does she want to meet me, too? What about if she doesn't want to meet me?*

I found out from Hannah's family that my youngest biological brother was living with MariJani in the mud hut. The emotion continued, and guilt started to kick in, *Why was I adopted and my siblings weren't?* Then sadness. *Why didn't she want to keep me? Was it because of the circumstances in which I was conceived? Was I a reminder of her trauma? Why could she care for the boys but not me?* Then more guilt, *Is she okay? Are they okay? How did they survive?* Then back to my urgent desire to meet them.

Through Facebook, Hannah and her parents were able to help get my parents in contact with the missionaries who took over the mission in Bukavu after my family moved to the United States. The new missionaries, Brenda, Dawn, and Dawn's husband, Bob, were in fact living in the same mission house my family used to live in. They were no longer part of African Christian Mission. They were now part of a faith-based non-profit called Heart for Central Africa, doing similar work to what my parents did thirty years prior.

The Democratic Republic of the Congo isn't a place that is easily accessible as a tourist. In order to get a visa to enter the county, one needs an invitation from a Congolese resident, then approval from the Congolese government. The visa is expensive and only valid for a certain amount of time after it's approved; the approval process can take a few months. Traveling to Bukavu is also a challenge because there isn't a commercial option to fly into eastern Congo, where Bukavu is located. To travel to Bukavu, one has to fly into neighboring Rwanda and walk across the Rwanda/Congo border.

Brenda, Dawn, and Bob, with the help of my parents' old friend Jean Pierre (who worked for the mission organization with my parents in the '80s and now works for Heart for Central Africa), managed to help my parents, my mom's cousin Cathy, and me over the next ten months with obtaining our visas and coordinating our travel plans to Bukavu.

To help ensure a positive trip if things with MariJani didn't go well, my parents, Cathy, and I also planned a safari in Kenya, a few days in Rwanda, and a week in Germany to visit my brother Ted who was living there at the time. All together the trip length would be a month.

After my parents and I made initial plans, I called my directors from work, Jon and Craig. Outside of the emotion I was experiencing, I was concerned about traveling for a month while successfully maintaining business with my clients and consultants. I wasn't sure if it would be possible or the smartest move for me, during what felt like a peak of my career. Here I was, mis-prioritizing and focusing on the minutiae of day-to-day work when my heart and soul were about to depart on an impeccable journey. Both Jon and Craig reminded me that before I am an employee, I am first a human and that I needed to focus on being present for myself and for my family.

My colleagues were extremely supportive and agreed to take care of all of my business for me so I wouldn't have to worry about missing meetings, emails, and phone calls. It was a relief to know I could go on what could be a life-changing trip and not have to worry about the daily stresses of work.

In late October, I was named a "40 Under 40 Business Leader in West Michigan" by *Grand Rapids Business Journal*. Upon receiving the award, a bio about me was published, where I conveyed my upcoming trip to meet my biological mother. The publication was eager to capture the story of me meeting MariJani in real time, which was just a few weeks away. The pressure of knowing many readers would be following the story added to the pressure I was experiencing. What if the trip went wrong? What if we couldn't find MariJani? What if she didn't want to meet me after we got there?

A couple of days before I left for the trip, my TEKsystems colleagues gave me $1,000 to give to Brenda, Dawn, and Bob to donate to locals who were in need of medical care. To provide a frame of reference, due to the extremely poor economy in the Congo, US$1,000 in Bukavu would have about the same value as $10,000 in America.

My biological mother, MariJani, holding me when I was about six months old.

Harkema family in Kenya: Eli, Ted, Josh, Heather, my mom, my dad, and me.

My mom, Jayn, and me while living in the Congo.

My dad, Ray, and me the day my adoption was official, September 1986.

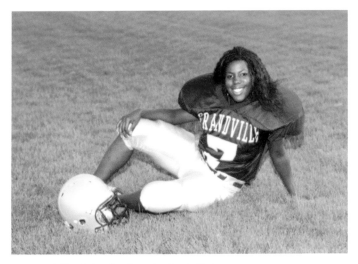

My Grandville High School varsity football photo.

Me with my parents, Ray and Jayn Harkema.

Me with my TEKsystems colleagues Kristen, Janey, Craig, and Allie.

Harkema family—parents, siblings, spouses, nieces, and nephews.

My biological mother, MariJani, and me the day we met, November 2015.

My dad holding his phone as MariJani video chats with me.

My mom holding her phone as MariJani video chats with me.

Laughs with friends Beth, Amy, Dave, and Janet at a favorite local restaurant, The Commons.

My dog, Teddy Roosevelt, shortly after I got him.

Friends Amy, Jonathan, Kerry, Melina, Charlsie, and Michelle celebrating my thirty-seventh birthday with me.

Christmas in the Congo 2022: my dad, biological brother Musa, me, MariJani, and mom.

Me delivering keynote, 2022. Background photo of MariJani holding me.

OUR INVITATION FROM THE CONGOLESE GOVERNMENT was accepted and our visas arrived. I remember tightly gripping my passport in my hand. On November 14, 2015, we embarked on a journey of a lifetime. The trip to Bukavu from Grand Rapids, including layovers, is about thirty-two hours: Grand Rapids, Michigan, to Atlanta, Georgia, to Amsterdam, Netherlands, to a fuel stop in Entebbe, Uganda, then to Kigali, Rwanda, to Cyangugu, Rwanda, and a walk over the rickety bridge which served as the border to Bukavu, Congo.

Flying to the Congo to meet my biological mother, felt like I was sitting at the top of the world's largest roller coaster. I had longed to ride it for years, its thrill excited me, its magnitude had intimidated me; I was terrified and nauseous. My apprehension was building, my anxiety was high; however, I knew I had to meet her. We all sat together in the middle row on the large plane, trying to chat, trying to read, trying to distract ourselves with a movie while all breathlessly smiling with nervous anticipation.

WE ARRIVED IN RWANDA timid, anxious, and eager. We carried our luggage and walked across the rickety bridge crossing into Bukavu, where we met Jean Pierre, who would escort us through the city. I was in complete and utter culture shock; Congo was not at all how I remembered it. The last time I was in Africa was in 2005, when I taught English at an AIDS orphanage in Kenya when I was twenty years old. Up to that point, I thought I had seen it all—in retrospect, Kenya was heavenly bliss in comparison to the Congo.

The infrastructure of Bukavu reminded me of an eerie mixture between the movies *Mad Max* and *The Book of Eli*. Parts of the city appeared postapocalyptic, in the midst of the slum, with dirt roads engulfing potholes the size of an entire vehicle. People walked in the road, barefoot, carrying anything they could balance on top of their heads and wrap around their arms, walking for miles, often with several children walking behind them, carrying all that they could fit in their hands or strapped to their backs.

There was no visible middle class—the only cars on the red-clay covered streets were newer-looking Mercedes, Toyotas, and police and UN vehicles. We bundled into a taxi Jean Pierre ordered for us. We passed malnourished residents wearing brightly patterned ripped clothing, selling food and other goods on the side of the road just to survive. Incomplete buildings appeared to have been constructed ten to twenty years prior, with construction halted in the middle of the project due to lack of funds. Homes that weren't in the slums were surrounded by tall brick walls topped with circular barbed wire for protection from thieves. Crime rates were extremely high, which meant women shouldn't be outside alone, especially at night. In contrast to the streets, the backdrop of the city was the most beautiful and lush landscape I had ever seen. Bright, vibrant, flourishing flowers and plants that were taller than me. The landscape was a canvas of greens, pinks, and purples—the land was radiant; it was a glimpse of heaven surrounding what looked like a poverty-stricken, postapocalyptic war zone.

The first night of our stay, Brenda told us of a couple who had just given birth to a baby and were stuck at the hospital because the hospital wouldn't release them until they paid for their labor and delivery costs. They couldn't afford it. The couple paid all they could but didn't have the rest; they were tormented and didn't know what they were going to do. I told Brenda about the money my colleagues had donated. Brenda asked if we could use some of the funds for the couple.

"Absolutely," I exclaimed. "How much do they need?"

Brenda sadly whispered, "Thirty-five dollars."

I was stunned . . . $35 for the hospital labor and delivery of a human child? I would pay that for dinner and drinks without even thinking about it. I then thought of the harsh reality of how hard my life could have been had I grown up here and how far the US dollar goes in Bukavu.

———————

THE NIGHT BEFORE WE WERE supposed to meet MariJani, my parents and I were all overwhelmed with emotion. My mom and dad knew how much this trip meant to me and were trying to remain positive, though glimpses of angst and despair came through. With fear in her eyes, my mom asked me in a shaky voice, "After tomorrow, will I still be your mom?"

My heart sank and felt like it had been pierced hearing those words; once again tears overflowed the surface of my eyelids as I began to rapidly wipe them away. With sincerity, I said, "Of course." My need to meet my biological mother didn't take away from my mom being my mom. I could only begin to imagine the worry she felt and the risk she was taking.

I had a restless night of tossing and turning, the worst sleep I had ever had. I woke up early, hours before my alarm. I couldn't lie in bed any longer. It was the morning I was supposed to meet my biological mother. We were staying in a guest house, much like a Westernized version of a bed and breakfast. Word had spread like crazy throughout Bukavu, Kidodobo, and the surrounding villages that I had returned to meet MariJani. Word had gotten to MariJani that I wanted to meet her, but I still didn't know how she felt about meeting me. Since my adoption was so rare, many of the locals remembered the White American family who adopted the Black African baby. Many of those same people were still there living in the villages; they were so intrigued and curious to see what the meeting with MariJani and me would be like that they came to witness it like it was a reality TV show. Old friends and acquaintances of my parents from thirty years ago were eager to be a part of the momentous day.

Jean Pierre arranged for MariJani to arrive at the guest house we were staying at. But she was late, and waiting for her to arrive seemed like an eternity. The fear crept back in; I thought she wasn't coming—what was I going to tell everyone? What would I say to the *Business Journal*? More doubts: perhaps she really didn't want to meet me, perhaps she gave me up and not my brothers for a reason. My mind raced as my heart anticipated; my face was blank, my voice was silent, I almost couldn't handle it any longer.

There was a brisk rustling at the front door of the guest house, and several people walked through and filled the room. My head quickly turned to the door; in amazement, I saw her... I *knew* her. Eyes bright and open, we both grinned from ear to ear and embraced each other tightly. She looked at me and in Swahili proclaimed, "My child. My child. My child."

MariJani speaks a tribal language called Mashi. Jean Pierre translated her Mashi into Swahili, then Dawn translated Swahili to English. Even though we spoke different languages, we have the same vocal inflections. The moment of seeing her and hearing those first words, "My child. My child. My child," all was perfect—everything made sense and I felt complete, whole. I belonged. Tears of joy streamed down everyone's faces, everyone except for MariJani and me; we just kept smiling. Our smiles almost identical, I discovered where my smile came from.

Standing next to MariJani were my two biological brothers, Mulume and Musa. Our connection was as if we had known each other for our entire lives. The older one, Mulume, is four years younger than me. He was twenty-six at the time, married with three kids. His wife and youngest baby daughter, Neema, were with him. *Neema* means grace, the same name as mine—it was as if it were a sign. Mulume didn't know of my existence, or my name, until just before we met. Mulume is a few inches taller than me, athletic build, much taller than Musa. Musa is sixteen years younger than me. He was single, living with MariJani in the mud hut. He is shorter, about the same height as MariJani, with a very slender build.

We all sat down on the couch in the living area of the guest house. I sat close to MariJani on the love seat. My mom, her cousin Cathy, and Mulume's wife sat adjacent to us on the other couch. Musa, Dawn, Brenda, and Chantal, who works for Heart for Central Africa, sat nearby. My dad proudly stood at the back of the room, recording each moment through a video camera he was holding. Through Jean Pierre and Dawn translating each word MariJani, my brothers, and I said, I thoughtfully and enthusiastically asked MariJani several questions about her life. I couldn't believe she had survived, beating so many odds. I learned my biological father wasn't someone Mari-Jani was in a relationship with, nor did she know him. I asked MariJani her age. Her current age was unclear because of the lack of access to hospitals or records; however, she showed me an ID card with a made-up birth date pressed into it. On the ID card, her nickname read Nsimire. I studied her ID card as if I were prepping for a test. Holding on to it tightly, reading everything aloud, over and over.

As I read the name, Nsimire, my mom nearly jumped out of her seat exclaiming, "That's my name! I mean, that's what they used to call me."

I was amazed and
overwhelmed to see
someone just like me, for
the first time in my life.

With my eyebrows scrunched together, I turned toward my mom. "What?" I questioned in confusion.

She continued, "Nsimire. That was my name when we lived here." Then it dawned on me like a lightbulb: my mom's name is Jayn, originally Jane, and my biological mother's name is MariJani, which translates to English as MaryJane. Both mothers have the same Westernized meaning of a name and the same nickname—I took it as another sign.

As we continued to converse, I began to grasp a fraction of what MariJani went through to survive and her desire for me to have a good life. It wasn't that she didn't want *me*, it was that she wanted better *for me*. During the Rwandan Genocide, rebel attacks often crossed into the area of Bukavu and its surrounding villages. Yet somehow MariJani lived through the attacks, the riots, the violence, and abuse; she fought diseases, malnutrition, starvation, and through it all still managed to stay alive, even without access to clean water. She was just grateful to be alive and have the divine opportunity to meet her child.

While sitting on the love seat, my arm beside hers, I looked down and noticed her arm and wrist were nearly identical to mine, just smaller. My eyes followed her arm, to her face, then captured her ear, noticing her ears looked just like mine, then her nose—just like mine, then also her eyes, filled with the same twinkle as mine. The way we moved and scooched back into our seat, also the same. I was amazed and overwhelmed to see someone just like me, for the first time in my life. We took several photos together, laughing and smiling in astonishment of all of our resembling mannerisms and features.

I brought MariJani and my biological brothers gifts; one of the gifts for MariJani included a photobook of big moments throughout my life. MariJani looked at each photo with incredible pride. While enjoying the gifts, we exchanged countless smiles and hugs. There were moments that didn't have words, just smiles, and in those moments, the smiles were enough. Mulume and Musa didn't know anything about the United States. When I gave them a handwritten greeting card in Swahili with the American flag on the card cover, they opened the envelope and glanced at the American flag, then turned it over to the backside of the card, confused about what was on the cover. The rectangle filled with white stars in a sea of blue, adjacent to red and white horizontal stripes meant nothing to them. The American flag was nothing they had ever seen before; however, they were proud to have a sister who lived and worked there.

MariJani proclaimed how proud she was of me and how I'd been living my life. She said, "Continue to do good work and help people."

I soaked in her words as they infiltrated into the depths of my soul.

I was home in my homeland, surrounded by the biology I came from. I gained a renewed sense of purpose, and I felt complete in who I was and why I was alive. I experienced a peace I had never felt before: peace meaning a state of tranquility or serenity; freedom from any strife or dissension; freedom of the mind from annoyance, distraction, anxiety, or obsession; a state of harmony. For the first time in my life, the anxiety of trying to fit in, not looking like anyone else in the room, hoping to be liked, or seeking others' approval wasn't even a thought that came into my mind. I was truly at peace and felt whole and complete—my mere existence was enough. *I was enough.*

After our conversations, we all sat at the dining table, continuing to laugh and smile while enjoying freshly baked bread and the best-tasting juicy, fresh tropical fruit and drinking bottled soda—a real treat my brothers especially enjoyed. Chantal and Jean Pierre laughed with us and helped translate. My mom

I was truly at peace
and felt whole and complete—
my mere existence was
enough. *I was enough.*

and dad joined the conversation, and they were relieved and also at peace. My mom and dad packed extra food for MariJani and Mulume to take to their homes. The guest house was filled with love and joy so thick it could seep through the cracks.

Mulume had a cellphone, so he and I exchanged phone numbers when the time came to say goodbye. I held MariJani tightly and told her I would come back to see her again. My heart was overwhelmed with joy and comfort; it was the happiest, most perfect day of my life. Jean Pierre and my parents hired a driver to bring MariJani home to Kidodobo. Before Mari-Jani got into the car, she whispered something to Dawn. Dawn's face dropped, and she quickly went to the taxi driver and whispered something in his ear. I was perplexed about what was happening as they drove away.

Dawn then told me MariJani disclosed to her that she was dying of malaria. She was happy to have lived her life and now that she had met me, she was at peace and ready to go. I immediately became angry. I finally got to meet her, and she was finally in my life; she couldn't die. Dawn had given the rest of the money from my colleagues' donation, $965, to the taxi driver and told him to take MariJani to the clinic to make sure she was given the best treatment. It was as if she were a celebrity receiving state-of-the-art health care. I was consumed with a whirlwind of emotion, and as we left for Kenya the next day, I kept anxiously wondering what was going to happen to Mari-Jani and prayed she would survive and be okay.

While on safari in Kenya, a few days later, I received a text message from Mulume. In Swahili, he said, "Mama MariJani is doing well. We thank God for you. You came to save us."

The treatment saved her life. I came to the Congo to meet my biological mother and say thank you for giving me up and giving me life—in return, I left the Congo helping to save my biological mother's life.

## TIPS FOR THOSE THINKING OF INTERNATIONALLY OR TRANSRACIALLY ADOPTING

- Take time to learn about the culture, background, and heritage of the adoptee prior to bringing the child into your family.

- Be open and honest about sharing the origin and adoption story with the adoptee.

- For the duration of the adoptee's life, continue to incorporate their culture, background, and heritage into their life and into your family.

- If the child is transracially adopted, the world won't always see your child as your child; they will see your child as their identity. It's important for your child to have their own sense of identity in addition to your family.

- If your child is struggling with their identity, don't take it personally. Be there to support them on their journey, offering safe and open conversations about what they are going through.

- Have access to therapy and/or social work as well as many resources. Encourage therapy as a safe, objective outlet for your child and the rest of your family.

- Create safe spaces of interaction for your child with other children and role models who are adopted.

**RECOMMENDED BOOKS FOR ADOPTIVE FAMILIES**

- *The Connected Child: Bring Hope and Healing to Your Adoptive Family* by Karyn B. Purvis, David R. Cross, and Wendy Lyons Sunshine

- *In Their Voices: Black Americans on Transracial Adoption* by Rhonda M. Roorda

- *What White Parents Should Know about Transracial Adoption: An Adoptee's Perspective on Its History, Nuances, and Practices* by Melissa Guida-Richards

CURIOSITY AND BRAVERY are sometimes very similar. I had to find the bravery to ask the right questions, on my time. There were several times throughout my life where my mom offered to share information about what my biological mother was like; however, I wasn't ready. I was too afraid. Over the course of time, my *need* to know if my biological mother was still alive became stronger and eventually led me around the globe. When you feel that urge to seek answers in your life, you may also find yourself taking journeys you didn't know you were capable of, and/or forming forever bonds that may change you and others.

# 9

# The Beauty in Belonging

"The opposite of belonging is fitting in... Belonging is belonging to yourself first. Speaking your truth, telling your story, and never betraying yourself for other people. True belonging doesn't require you to change who you are; it requires you to be who you are."

**BRENÉ BROWN**

EMBRACING THE DIVERSITY of my identities gave me the strength to break down my own internal barriers instead of hiding from them. I had harbored so much anger and sadness over the adversities I had faced since childhood. For thirty years of my life, I wished I was someone else, anyone else. After the experience of meeting my biological mother, I no longer viewed my identities as my shame. Instead, I viewed my identities as my superpower. I couldn't pick and choose the identities I wanted to be, internally or externally. I couldn't accept myself until I accepted all aspects of myself.

Brené Brown's book *Braving the Wilderness* impacted me greatly, especially the chapter-opening quote. When I tried to change who I was for other people's expectations, I was losing myself and who I am supposed to be. For years, I thought I wasn't enough, based on other people's expectations, but I have since learned I am more than enough because of His creations. I believe in a God who doesn't make mistakes—we are His creation. In believing He doesn't make mistakes, I believe we have all been created with uniqueness, which makes us valuable in this world. We all have traits, characteristics, and perspectives that nobody else has, and the world is better for it.

Accepting and embracing my identities unlocked the power of being able to use my voice to advocate for myself and for others. I was no longer submissive to other people's opinions and learned how to craft my own voice while growing confident in myself and my abilities. I let go of the insecurities and fear which held me captive and in turn became proud of all aspects of who I am. We have been created as we are for a reason. We aren't able to be real with others until we are real with ourselves. Our voices are most powerful when we are our truest, authentic selves.

During difficult times, it is easy for us to question why we are going through certain challenges or adversities. We later find when sharing our experiences that our courage is what others need in order to connect, learn, grow, and know they aren't alone. I learned by embracing my diversity. I was able to use my experiences to have empathy for others, build meaningful connections, and provide opportunities for greater inclusion.

Meeting my biological mother and helping to save her life completely rocked my world. The closest person I am biologically related to, the closest person I share the same blood with, who I thought was dead for thirty years, was alive. She was alive because I helped save her life after she gave me up to help save mine! I was forever changed. I couldn't unlive what I had just experienced; there was no going back. I was a new version of myself, with a renewed sense of purpose.

I had no idea what MariJani endured just for me to exist on this earth. I grew to have empathy and began to see experiences and perspectives outside of my own. Seeing my face reflected in my biological mother's face helped me embrace all elements of my identity—not just what is seen on the surface, but everything that encompasses me, from my sexual orientation to my skin color. It helped me be grounded in knowing myself and be confident in who I am. Following the times I wished I wasn't

**"**

We aren't able to
be real with others
until we are real
with ourselves.

**"**

alive, I then understood God's plan for me. Knowing who I was and what drove me helped me understand others better, by being able to see them for who they are, in addition to their experiences and perspectives outside of my own.

In discovering my purpose to help others live and work more authentically, I learned that my experiences and adversities weren't just for me. My experiences and adversities were for those who have felt alone, for those who had been silenced, and for those who need the courage to be resilient and keep going. I knew what it was like to feel excluded, and I knew the power of inclusive leadership that propels us to be our truest selves and reach our potential. It solidified my desire to have a leadership role in diversity, equity, and inclusion.

We all have a part to play in increasing equity and inclusion in our world. Systemic injustices require systemic solutions. We all have a part in sharing and receiving open communication, exercising emotional intelligence, and increasing equity and inclusion in our environments. The work of diversity, equity, and inclusion never stops, and, yes, the work takes work. The work is continuous and requires accountability—accountability to ourselves and to our peers. The work takes intentionality for us to be able to truly see others and for us to allow ourselves to authentically be seen. When we see others, we are able to value them, understand them, empathize with them, and leverage equity in order to encourage and empower equal outcomes, even when their experiences and journeys are much different from our own. We aren't going to boil the ocean today; however, we can start increasing equity and inclusion in our world today. If you see an injustice or discriminatory behavior or action happening near you, instead of disengaging or turning the other way, confront the situation and say something, especially if you have privilege in the situation.

Of course, try to remain safe and don't put yourself in harm's way. In a workplace or educational or social environment, if you see something, say something. Your voice is powerful. Being intentional about implementing inclusive and equitable practices can impact one person. Helping just one person creates a ripple effect. Ripple effects create a wave. Waves create change. We have the ability to change the world; it starts with one person.

---

I HAD BEEN WORKING IN diversity recruiting and account management for three years at TEKsystems when a leadership role within the company, as a regional diversity and inclusion manager, opened up. The role was a traveling position with corporate headquarters, to help support some of the company's largest clients, including Fortune 100 corporations, while supporting the company's field offices across North America in internal and external diversity, equity, and inclusion initiatives and training. The role seemed perfect; it was literally everything I wanted to be doing. I aspired to be the type of inclusive leader Alex, Jon, and Craig were for me. I was passionate about creating and fostering environments of inclusivity by encouraging others to live more authentically and have the opportunity to reach their potential inside and outside of the workplace.

When the regional diversity and inclusion manager role opened up, I quickly networked with executives throughout the company whom I had built strong relationships with throughout the years. I submitted my resume for the position. Within a couple of weeks, I received a request for an in-person interview at the corporate headquarters in Baltimore. I was thrilled; the stars were aligning. This position was everything I wanted. I had thoroughly prepared for the interview, spending time with executives representing various sectors of the company to make sure I wasn't missing anything and to practice all the "How would you handle..." "What would you do in this situation?" and "What are your greatest strengths and weaknesses?" questions.

On the days leading up to the interview, I received emails and text message affirmations from various leaders stating, "You're going to crush the interview," and "You were made for this!" I believed the affirmations and even listened to Post Malone's "Congratulations" on repeat for the entire flight to Baltimore.

I arrived in Baltimore and confidently entered the conference room for the interview. I was greeted by two DEI executives, Michelle and Franklin, who were also my mentors who had been grooming me in DEI, training me, and leading me in running our national pride employee resource group program. I felt like I overprepared for each anticipated question. I recall answering each question with a confident yet peaceful grin. The interview flew by like a breeze. It felt so smooth that my entire trip for the interview felt like a vacation. At the end of the interview, Michelle and Franklin told me there were other candidates in the mix and they would be making decisions in a week. I thought I nailed it. I wasn't very concerned about the other candidates and thought I was the perfect candidate for the role.

Each day after that, I nervously and repetitiously checked my email and frantically answered every call, hoping it was Michelle or Franklin delivering me good news. Friday afternoon came; recognizing the area code on my caller ID, I grabbed my cellphone and sprinted into an open boardroom to take the call. I didn't get the role. Their words kept repeating like a broken record. I didn't understand; I asked them to repeat it. I didn't get the role. I was confused and upset—devasted. How did I not get the job? I wanted to lash out, but I knew I had to keep myself professional and composed. "What do you mean? I'd love feedback on the areas I fell short in." Their feedback was that I was weak in two areas: investing in others and driving client development.

I received the feedback and frankly, I thought it was BS. I left the office and sobbed in my car. It didn't make sense to me. My anger turned into rage. I spent the weekend at my favorite local gay bar, The Apartment, indulging in cocktails and pizza from Peppino's—living a sob story. By the time Monday came around, I couldn't do it. Still filled with anger, I called into work for a personal day.

My friend Amy was a very close, supportive friend who decided to play hooky with me. That day was a lunar eclipse, and we pampered ourselves with pedicures, went to a VIP eclipse party, went out for lunch, and then hit up a local happy hour. The day was one of the most fun days I had ever had in my life; however, I had to let myself feel through the pain. The only way through it, was *through* it. I had been so used to stuffing down my emotions and sweeping my sadness under the rug. That day, I had to live through the emotions to fully feel them— all of them. I felt the anger, the hurt, the disappointment, the shock, the sadness. Even when we don't agree with feedback we are being given, I believe there can be a bit of truth to someone's perception of us. Other people's perception of us is their reality. Learn from those who can give you wisdom, without compromising your purpose and your voice.

I lived through all of the emotions, including the guilt that crept in later that evening. Months prior, I had left my biological mother and brothers in poor health, who barely survived living through civil unrest in what looked like a postapocalyptic war-torn country, and here I was, wallowing in my sadness over not getting my dream when truly I already had a really great job.

I realized I needed to work though my sadness, so I dissected the interview feedback I received and came to the realization that I needed to work on my weak areas, even when I couldn't see it at first.

I came to work on Tuesday, ready to work—ready to work and grow in the areas I wasn't strong in. I sought out leaders who excelled in my weak areas to mentor me in their strengths. I shared my feedback with them and that I wanted to learn from them. I knew this growth opportunity could take months and that my dream job was already filled with one of the other candidates. I had to equip myself to be the best I could be in my current role, not for the reason of a promotion, but for the sake of the job. I focused on gaining more experience in the areas I wasn't as versed in. I leaned on my previous and new mentors to help me see areas of opportunity where I could grow. I took on side projects that weren't a part of my day-to-day job duties in order to execute in those areas of opportunity. I took the feedback of not having enough client experience and created a stretch assignment that would involve ten major clients of the West Michigan office.

I was still disappointed in not getting the role, but my pride wasn't going to get me anywhere, so I learned how to swallow it and instead build new client development skills. I kept grinding and remained focused on building skills in inclusive leadership and client development for the next three months. I invested in my team and new recruiters by helping them achieve their goals and drive their performance. All of the members on my team achieved their performance goals, and I grew my performance at the same time. I didn't do any of that because I was asked to; I did it to get better.

Character is who you are when you think nobody is watching. Growing in client development increased my work ethic and business acumen. Investing in others increased my inclusive leadership skills. I didn't think another diversity and inclusion leadership role would open up, but surprisingly, Michelle and Franklin reached back out to me to tell me another role opened a few months later. The extra work I did to go grow as a leader and go above and beyond equipped me with the skills and experience to be ready for the role. I submitted my resume for the new regional manager role and began prepping for a potential interview. When I least expected it, without even interviewing, I was promoted to be a regional diversity and inclusion manager!

For those of you who have been in a similar situation, who've interviewed for a role and didn't get it, don't think it's over. You never know when the next opportunity will be available, even if it was missed the first time. As cliché as it sounds, one door closing really can create opportunities for another door or window or perspective to open when we least expect it. When we get so set on our own goals and our own plan, God, or the universe, or whatever higher power you may believe in could have something even greater than our imagination has in store for us.

───────

AFTER MY PARENTS AND I met MariJani, my mom and dad came into the realization of their purpose. It was around the same time I did, too. They both realized there was work they could do for the people in my hometown, Bukavu, Congo, similar to the work they did thirty years prior. About a year after we met MariJani, my mom and dad were so emotionally moved that, in 2016, they moved to the Congo, where they now live half of the year, helping to run a faith-based non-profit called Heart for Central Africa–Building Bukavu (buildingbukavu.org).

My parents work with Brenda, another American who founded an organization called Tracy's Heart, which is under the umbrella of Heart for Central Africa. Tracy's Heart was started as a way to help marginalized women, such as survivors of abuse, sex trafficking, and rape, due to twenty years of violence and civil war. The faith-based mission helps restore hope by teaching the women about God's love and self-love. They equip the women with entrepreneurial and business skills by teaching them a trade or art to run their own micro businesses. The skills the women receive allow them to make a financial living, put food on the table, and send their children to school.

In addition to my parents supporting Tracy's Heart, the needs of locals who have been imprisoned have become known. Unless an inmate has relatives or friends nearby to bring food, there is little to eat. Many are not from that area, therefore starvation will be the result. My parents, together with local men and women, began a feeding program that contributes three meals a week to all the inmates. They also provide them with spiritual guidance, love, and encouragement.

War, disease, and poverty often leave children orphaned and homeless. As a result, Tracy's Heart has opened a school for those children. The school has been added to the feeding program my parents help support, providing a meal every day to the school-children. In that program, an investment of merely US$8.00 provides a child with nourishing meals six days a week, for a month. My parents' work with Heart for Central Africa literally saves thousands of lives and often helps support men, women, and homeless, orphaned children find belonging and purpose.

During the same time period of my parents' work in the Congo, I learned that life isn't just about accomplishing our professional goals. It's also about accomplishing our personal goals. One of the goals I had after I met my biological mother was to buy her a house. She had been living in a mud hut for her entire life. I experienced walking on the same red-clay earth she had slept on every night. Soon after my mom and dad moved to Bukavu, through the help of their local friends, they were able to reconnect with my biological mother. By partnering with my parents and their friends with Heart for Central Africa–Building Bukavu, I was able to get my biological mother a house. She had never had a kitchen or dining table before, and my brother had never had his own room, or even a bed. A house meant safety, warmth, sanitation, and the ability to make and store food.

MariJani now has a bed, with a real mattress to sleep on. My brother has his own bed. MariJani has a cooking area in the back of the house with a firepit where she can make food. My mom and dad bought her a dining table, chairs, and pots and pans. Through my mom and dad's work with Building Bukavu, I have the honor of financially supporting my biological mother for all of her needs and desires for the rest of her life. She gave me life; the least I can do is give her some back. At a time when her future was bleak, she is now healthy and living her best life, a life beyond her imagination.

On the day MariJani and I met for the first time, my dad was recording the moment with a brand-new video camera, which I received as a gift from Craig at TEKsystems. The first words she said to me in Swahili, "My child. My child. My child," continued to sing in my head like a sweet melody for several months. After MariJani was settled in her new home, enjoying her new life, I wanted to get a tattoo as a permanent commemoration and celebration of the special bond we share. I first shared the idea with my mom, Jayn, and she agreed. It was a beautiful sentiment. On my right forearm, I got the soundwave of MariJani's voice joyfully exclaiming, "My child. My child. My child," in Swahili tattooed on my skin. A forever reminder and an additional piece of her, as a piece of me, always bringing me a smile, even on the worst days.

My mom and biological mother share a special, beautiful bond—almost uncanny—a selfless, shared love of their daughter. My mom and dad living in the Congo also gives my biological mother and me the ability to belong together, by now having a long-standing relationship. We are able to remain in communication by video chatting with one another on my parents' cellphones, since my parents are the few there that my biological mother has access to with an international phone plan, electricity, and Wi-Fi. I can't imagine what it is like for her to be able to video chat with her biological daughter, across the world, in real time. However, her radiant joy shining through the screen of the phone says it all. Through two-layered interpretation (English translated to Swahili, and Swahili translated into Mashi), in one of our recent conversations, MariJani rejoiced and said, "When you were a baby, I didn't know if I'd ever see you again. I'm so happy to see you now."

My heart grieves and praises the stark contrast of the trauma my biological mother must have lived through, and the horror in having to give me away, with the full life and radiant joy she now has. I imagine that existing in each moment is beyond what she could previously comprehend. After thirty years of thinking she was dead, I cherish every second of her existence. In each video chat conversation, through each translated word, I grasp for time to hold still as I study each moment, each of her movements and all of her mannerisms, finding myself in the reflection. Countless questions swirl in my mind—so many aspects of her I'd still love to learn about, so many things I want to say—but the only words that come to the surface are, "I love you, Mama MariJani."

MY CAREER AT TEKSYSTEMS made it possible for me to have the financial ability to support my biological mother—I was able to pay for her home, health care, and day-to-day needs. After bleak and dark times, when I didn't know it would be possible, I experienced beauty in finding and accepting belonging within myself. My parents found belonging in a new venture, Heart for Central Africa–Building Bukavu, which continues to impact many lives. My biological mother and mom found belonging in one another, a beauty so rare. And I found beauty and belonging with my biological mother. Even in the dark times, opportunities that we hadn't imagined can arise in our lives when we are least expecting it. There is beauty in belonging.

**TEN RECOMMENDED BOOKS FOR CONTINUED LEARNING IN EQUITY AND INCLUSION**

- *So You Want to Talk About Race* by Ijeoma Oluo

- *Uncomfortable Conversations with a Black Man* by Emmanuel Acho

- *How to Be an Antiracist* by Ibram X. Kendi

- *Inclusion: Diversity, the New Workplace & the Will to Change* by Jennifer Brown

- *How to Be an Inclusive Leader: Your Role in Creating Cultures of Belonging Where Everyone Can Thrive* by Jennifer Brown

- *I'm Still Here: Black Dignity in a World Made for Whiteness* by Austin Channing Brown

- *Showing Up: How Men Can Become Effective Allies in the Workplace* by Ray Arata

- *The Hate U Give*, a novel by Angie Thomas

- *Just Mercy: A Story of Justice and Redemption* by Bryan Stevenson

- *Atlas of the Heart: Mapping Meaningful Connection and the Language of Human Experience* by Brené Brown

**TEN RECOMMENDED MOVIES FOR CONTINUED LEARNING IN EQUITY AND INCLUSION**

- *The Hate U Give*
- *Crash*
- *Fruitvale Station*
- *When They See Us*
- *I Am Sam*
- *Paris Is Burning*
- *13th*
- *Milk*
- *Wonder*
- *CODA*

# 10

# Courage over Comfort

"Believe in something, even if it means sacrificing everything."

**COLIN KAEPERNICK**

GROWTH DOESN'T come out of comfort. I was comfortable in my career, and I was comfortable in my life, but I had the urge to make an even greater impact in my career, even if it was uncomfortable. Former Facebook COO Sheryl Sandberg states, "Careers are not ladders, but jungle gyms... If I had planned out my career... I would have missed my career." The same goes for me. There were many sideways turns, opportunities, leaps, challenges, and obstacles throughout my career I didn't plan on but provided me the chance to learn more, grow more, and gain more.

In 2018, I traveled for forty-three weeks of the year for work at TEKsystems. I gained a lot of experience consulting, training, and public speaking on diversity, equity, and inclusion–related topics for some of the world's largest Fortune 100 corporations; however, I mourned not having a life of simple pleasures like happy hours with friends, dating, family get-togethers, sleeping in my own bed, and the chance to have a puppy.

An opportunity presented itself to be the diversity and inclusion director at a global craft brewery, headquartered in Grand Rapids, Michigan—an industry with a history of a lack of diversity, equity, and inclusion work. The brewery was faced with two conflicts based on discrimination. The first was with the LGTBQ+ community when the brewery initially posted on social media in support of the community, announcing they would be leaving a local chamber organization that publicly endorsed a gubernatorial candidate who was vocally against same-sex marriage. Nine days later, the brewery retracted this statement and stayed in the chamber. The second was an ongoing federal racial discrimination lawsuit against the brewery in which a former Black male employee sued the brewery for perpetrating a racist culture. One allegation, publicly proven true under oath, stated the incident of a White manager calling the former Black employee the N-word, without any disciplinary repercussion. The ongoing internal racial and LGBTQ+ conflicts and allegations of discrimination severely impacted the brewery's reputation with the Black, Brown, and LGBTQ+ communities.

My personal experience and credibility within the local Black, Brown, and LGBTQ+ communities, along with my professional experience in diversity, equity, and inclusion, made me highly sought after for the position. For me, the opportunity meant a work-life balance where I could actually have a life. While it was a pay cut from my position at TEKsystems, it was still a stable six-figure salary that allowed me to have a comfortable lifestyle, and, most importantly, the position was an opportunity for me to make a difference in the craft beer industry—something not many people were doing in the United States in 2019. Plus, I mean, come on, working at a brewery sounded fun!

DEI-related positions are often referred to as "the Lord's work." We are often brought into harassment, racist, sexist, homophobic situations to be the savior: prevent a lawsuit, help settle a lawsuit, resolve an issue, save the image or reputation of the organization, change the narrative, build an inclusive culture, hire a more diverse team, and help grown adults re-learn the principles they learned in kindergarten—how to play in the sandbox with others. DEI work is often unrecognized when things are going well within an organization, and then it's put under a microscope when thing aren't going well within the organization.

I knew the risks of taking the position with the brewery, but I also knew growth doesn't come from comfort. After accepting the position, many of the local news and national craft brewery–focused media headlines were rolling in. There was a lot of praise, but there was also a lot of negativity. A few people who I thought were close friends referred to me as a "sellout" and "one-hit wonder" on blogs and social media upon accepting the position, and somehow believed my Blackness and my queerness were negated from my existence. The more we grow in our career, the more critics we are going to have. I received a lot of criticism from people who were more interested in throwing rocks from the sidelines than from people who were actually doing the work.

At one point, I was the only woman and only person of color on the leadership team. The pressure was intense, but I had been used to pressure and was used to being "the only one of my kind" in corporate environments. We accomplished a lot in our internal processes and external community engagement partnerships with underrepresented and marginalized communities and organizations. However, policy change and more equitable processes and communications felt like two steps forward, one step back, a tug-of-war between support and resistance from leadership.

The media attention of the DEI work we were doing was growing from a local reach to national attention, so again, all of the praise and all of the criticism. I was often internally and externally positioned as a scapegoat for the fallouts and mishandlings of the racial discrimination lawsuit, even though the lawsuit was filed the year before I was hired there. As the criticism became overwhelming, I let the opinions of others get to me. Friends, who I soon learned were fake friends, were falling out of my life like sand running through my fingers. I even tried to hold on to them, but I just couldn't.

In an incident that may or may not have been related, after a brewery-associated fallout with a local community organization, someone maliciously stole thousands of dollars and personal belongings from me. I was also verbally assaulted by someone with a vendetta against the brewery because they were personally upset I was in the role. My work life was suddenly one blow immediately after another. I felt so defeated. I had taken this job so I could have a life, but the opposite was happening—my work was infringing upon nearly all aspects of my life.

I took others' negative opinions and criticisms to heart, to the point where I began getting panic attacks. Hives from anxiety began to cover my body. It almost destroyed me. I didn't know how to communicate what I was going through. I was under attorney-client privilege with the allegations of the lawsuit and the topic at large was very polarizing within my social circles. Through the turmoil of it all, I kept coming back to knowing I was standing my ground and following my purpose in doing the work. I believed in the work, and I believed in what needed to be done—even when it wasn't popular, even when it wasn't comfortable.

On one night of dreaded agony, on my way to Aruba for a solo getaway, I discovered and started reading Brené Brown's *Daring Greatly*. The book was recommended to me by Michelle at TEKsystems, but I hadn't given myself a moment to read it

until now. The night before I left for Aruba, I watched Brené
Brown's Netflix special, *The Call to Courage*. I was moved and
inspired, hungry, wanting more. Sitting on the flight to Aruba,
I downloaded the book. *Daring Greatly* focuses on Theodore
Roosevelt's 1910 speech known as "The Man in the Arena":

> It is not the critic who counts; not the man who points out
> how the strong man stumbles, or where the doer of deeds
> could have done them better. The credit belongs to the man
> who is actually in the arena, whose face is marred by dust
> and sweat and blood; who strives valiantly; who errs, who
> comes short again and again, because there is no effort with-
> out error and shortcoming; but who does actually strive to
> do the deeds; who knows great enthusiasms, the great devo-
> tions; who spends himself in a worthy cause; who at the best
> knows in the end, the triumph of high achievement, and
> who at the worst, if he fails, at least fails while daring greatly,
> so that his place shall never be with those cold and timid
> souls who neither know victory nor defeat.

I was the man in the arena, giving it everything I had, sacrificing friends, allowing the critics to have my power. But like an
epiphany, I realized it's not the critics who count. I no longer
was going to let the critics' voices, opinions, or criticisms count.
I had to stay true to myself, to live my truth and not compro-
mise my work.

I had become obsessed with my career and what people
thought of my career, and it was causing an excess of anxiety
and panic attacks. I committed myself to establishing healthy
boundaries from a social and relationship perspective. I realized I needed an outlet and a safe space that was separate from
my career, something else I could invest in and have fun with,
something that wasn't a person, something that was an escape

and a reminder that it's not the critic who counts. I needed something fulfilling, something that couldn't let me down, and something that I could love and spend time with. Something like a puppy.

While sitting on the beach in Aruba, reading *Daring Greatly*, I would occasionally take a break from the deep dive of my book, while sipping my frosted Miami Vice, a strawberry daiquiri mixed with piña colada, and check what was happening in the world of Facebook. While scrolling through my newsfeed, I saw the cutest photos of apricot-colored mini goldendoodle puppies sitting inside and beside silver-studded blue leather luggage bags. They were great photographs of beautiful fur babies. Naturally, my heart melted. The post was from my friend Larry, whose sister Kelley was searching for forever homes for her dog's new litter.

Since working at TEKsystems, I had longed for a dog. My niece Leah, an avid dog lover, would share her dog books with me when I went over to my sister's house. Leah and I would dream about what kind of dog we would each desire to have one day. Living in a high-rise apartment downtown, it only made sense to me, with my limited space, to have a small dog. I also loved the concept of being able to carry a dog in my purse, so those Facebook photos of little dogs peeking out from the luggage really got me. Learning that I had developed allergies over the years, I was also keen on having a hypoallergenic dog who didn't shed. Leah and I loved reading about goldendoodles' social temperaments, which they inherit from golden retrievers, and their quick-learning skills and smart abilities, which they inherit from poodles.

When I saw those mini goldendoodle puppies on Larry's post, I just knew one of those puppies was for me. I was home more and ready to invest in something aside from my career, something that would be a positive addition to my life. I reached out to him to let him know I was interested in putting a deposit down for a puppy. Larry put me in touch with Kelley. After I came back from Aruba, I sent Kelley an email on May 29, 2019, telling her why I was interested in adding a mini goldendoodle to my life and what it would mean to me:

> Kelley,
>
> I have worked a lot and have sacrificed a lot in my life for my career. I've realized after a recent vacation that I need to pause and enjoy life. I have a lot of love to give and time to spend with a puppy. I'm not in a relationship, nor do I have other obligations. My work is very flexible, less than a five-minute walk from home. I can bring him to work and walk him throughout the day. I have allergies and specifically wanted a mini goldendoodle. Having a mini goldendoodle is a second chance at life and love. I want the responsibility to care for something. I have the resources to enroll him in puppy school. I am ready to love and not spend my life alone.

The next week, Kelley and I met in person, and I got the puppy! I instinctively named him Teddy Roosevelt and fittingly, he looks just like a teddy bear. When I held him for the first time, I knew he was going to be safe and loved, and that my life would be more filled with joy with him in my home.

All of this meant I had a much better outlook on my role, another example of how when we're our fully realized selves, professional work is positively impacted. The critics were still guffawing, but I wasn't as bothered. I took each day one day at a time. Coming home from work to play and snuggle with Teddy also made things much better. I took him everywhere with me—friends' houses, the patio at a local gay bar, The Apartment, festivals, and even the grocery store. A dog's unconditional love can make the worst day the best day.

---

AFTER I HAD BEEN IN THE BREWERY ROLE for ten months, on Monday, October 21, 2019, up-to-date transcripts of a leaked ongoing deposition from the lawsuit hit national media. The *Washington Post* headline read, "'I Don't Know His DNA': Craft Brewery Manager Says He Can't Confirm Black Employee's Race in Discrimination Lawsuit." A headline from *Newsweek* exclaimed, "Leaked Deposition Shows General Manager of [the Brewery] Saying He Does Not Know If Barack Obama Is Black." NBC's headline read, "Black Michigan Man Says He Was Called the N-Word, Fired from Brewing Company."

Seeing the headlines made my heart fall to the pit of my stomach. I literally felt sick. The headlines were true. They were all true, which perhaps made me feel even worse. I knew that manager the headlines referred to; in fact, I had known him for years, since my law firm days. To me, the transcripts read like the manager was being told to answer the questions a certain way, with blatant disregard to race, to protect the brewery in the lawsuit. Outside of feeling sick, I felt angered, wondering, *Why would someone allow their voice to be influenced that much, to their own detriment?* Within days of the transcripts hitting the media, the manger was let go. It looked like he said what company leadership wanted him to say, and then they let him go, like a pawn.

My anger turned into "fight or flight." I knew we had to do something. Outraged, I conversed with others in leadership. "We can't let this be our reputation. We can't believe in what the manager said. We can't let the public believe we support what the manager said. We have to say something. We have to acknowledge this. We have to apologize."

Boycotts came rolling in: major grocery retailers, bars, and restaurants made statements of no longer supporting the brewery. By the next day, sales immediately plummeted by upwards of a million dollars, and each day after that. In meetings, I presented a plan, identical to the plan I presented in my interview, on how to increase our reputation and create an inclusive culture. I urged leadership to take accountability and responsibility, apologize for what was said under oath, and acknowledge the importance of seeing and valuing someone's race and identity. The leadership team didn't take my advice. They didn't want my advice. In short, their answer was, "No, we aren't going to do that. We will prevail in court."

I was thrown into the media, while our leadership, stakeholders, and community urged me to defend the brewery's position. The uproar of all the critics went into high gear. I went from feeling alone in a cave to instantly feeling like I was on a sinking ship in the eye of the storm in the middle of the ocean.

Filled with shock and utter disappointment, I was barely hanging on by a thread. Everything about the situation—the brewery's response to the leaked deposition, the harm they were causing to Black and Brown communities, and the complete disregard of my expertise—was causing stress on my personal life and identity. From my perspective, their pride and ego were sabotaging my credibility and reputation as an executive in the field of diversity, equity, and inclusion.

I was a thirty-four-year-old, single, Black female executive. I didn't come this far and work this hard, and risk this much, to have only come this far. It's easy for us to have faith and courage when things are going smoothly. The true test of our faith and courage comes when we have an opportunity to stand up for what we believe in. The opportunity to live our truth and show up, continuing to operate in the darkest hour, even when we feel like we are the only ones standing. I prayed and meditated for direction, leaned on my parents for wisdom, connected with a few close friends for support, and snuggled with Teddy for comfort.

The true test of our
faith and courage comes
when we have an opportunity
to stand up for what
we believe in.

I DID SOME DEEP REFLECTION with Brené Brown's *Daring Greatly* and *Braving the Wilderness*, and I remained centered on my purpose: to help others live and work more authentically, even if and when I felt like I was standing alone. The brewery had clout in Grand Rapids. Because of them and many other prominent breweries, Grand Rapids was voted "Beer City USA" in 2012.

Many people are afraid to speak out against powerful organizations. This was the time where I was either going to stand up for what was right and stand up for equity or sit down and be quiet and swallow the status quo of Black and Brown voices and discriminatory experiences being silenced. How could I live my purpose when other people's actions were hindering my work and overshadowing the change I thought I was there to create?

Have you felt halted or limited by other people's opinions? Have others' actions and beliefs inhibited your ability to fully do your job or your ability to live your purpose? If so, how did you handle it and what did you do? How do you get back to your "reason why"? Focusing on my "why" and what led me to the role to begin with helped me refocus on my "how," in terms of what I was going to do next. I took the position at the brewery to create an impact in an industry where diversity, equity, and inclusion work hadn't traditionally or historically been done; to help build an inclusive environment; and to help others live and work more authentically.

After an annual leadership budget meeting, I had inquired with executive leadership about my DEI budget for the upcoming year, and the director's unfiltered response was, "We only need your role for the press. We may not need your role next year."

I was stunned. Alarmed, as if I had heard something I was not supposed to hear, but ready to seek truth, I brought it to the attention of my boss, the head of the leadership team. He responded by saying, "That isn't true. I'm not sure why they would say that."

And then it all made sense: I was sure I was hired as a prop, as a pawn, as a gold star, not for my voice, not for my work, not for my experience, but to make the brewery look good for the press, amidst a lawsuit, before the forthcoming acquisition by a larger brewery.

All the while, during the fallouts of the mishandlings of the lawsuit, it was brought to my attention that other current and former brewery employees of marginalized identities, including Black, Latino, and transgender people, were being discriminated against at the brewery and were silenced after they brought their experiences to leadership's attention. I knew what it felt like to be silenced. I lived through the debilitating submission of allowing others to have my voice and my power. It was time I stood up and took my voice back, not just for me, but for others who had been silenced. I needed my voice to rise to allow others to be heard and seen.

In Brené Brown's *The Gifts of Imperfection*, she states, "Only when we are brave enough to explore the darkness will we discover the infinite power of our light."

----

ON FRIDAY, OCTOBER 25, 2019, I made the most terrifying decision I'd ever made: I resigned from the position without having another job lined up. I first resigned directly to the leadership team, then immediately after, with the advice of an attorney and public relations firm to avoid any potential defamation from the brewery, and to protect my narrative and credibility on all of my social media channels, I publicly posted my resignation letter. I posted this alongside an homage to a Nike ad, a black-and-white photograph of my face with the words of Colin Kaepernick overtop, spanning my cheekbones, "Believe in something, even if it means sacrificing everything."

Friday, October 25, 2019
Dear [brewery] Leadership Team,

Diversity is everything we bring to the table. Inclusion is ensuring we have a seat and a voice at the table. I knew what I signed up for regarding the lawsuit when I joined [the brewery]. I have supported [the brewery] each step of the way. I also know I signed up to represent an organization that believes in its people, an organization that believes its people are family. I believed in [the brewery] with every-thing I have. I believed in [the brewery] to the extent of sacrificing my personal life, my safety, my friends, rela-tionships with several community partners, and my health. The case study I created and interview process in which I was hired upon drew specific measures to increase [the brewery's] reputation in diversity and inclusion and regain the trust of the LGBTQ+ and People of Color communities. During my course of employment since January 2019, I have repeatedly given suggestions on how to build our rep-utation and listen to our employees who have been on the front lines. This week alone, I have repeatedly given explicit feedback on how to increase our reputation and increase our narrative, media reputation, and morale with employees. This feedback I have given is also the exact same feedback that credible public relations firms have given, which you blatantly disagreed with. In every conversation and with every action, you've been most concerned with winning the lawsuit. You are most concerned with the ego of "winning" than you are about the loss of customers, loss of reputation, and loss of employees' well-being. That does not exemplify the [the brewery's] principles of family, community, authenticity, dedication, humility, positivity, purposeful progress, diversity, and inclusion. We, as a company, didn't have to be at the place we are at now. If the voice of a diversity and inclusion director was heard, headlines would read much differently. We had the opportunity to be the hero in how we could have addressed this situation; instead, we have lost the trust of the community, many of our accounts, and many of our own employees. The prioritization of diversity and inclusion begins at the top. We are not experiencing a staff issue; we are experiencing a leadership issue. Inclusion is ensuring we have a seat and a voice at the table. Your actions have explicitly shown you are more interested in the optics of my face than the impact of my voice. I have dedicated myself to a life and career of equity, ethics, integrity, and morals. I cannot represent a company that doesn't stand for the same. Ego and greed will destroy an organization's brand and reputation. This is my two-week resignation as [the brewery's] diversity and inclusion director. My last day with [the brewery] will be Friday, November 8, 2019.

I wish you all the best,
Graci Harkema

I chose to use my voice to publicly stand up for what I believe in and to stand up for integrity, morals, and ethics and what is right, not just for me, but for others who didn't have a voice. I didn't know if I would be blacklisted from the beer industry or blacklisted from the city of Grand Rapids for that matter. All I knew was that I had to stay grounded in my faith and drive toward my "why." I was inspired by Dr. Martin Luther King Jr., who said, "The time is always right to do what is right."

Immediately after my resignation, with the anticipation of wanting to have a drink, or three, that night, I ordered an Uber to meet my parents at one of our favorite local restaurants, The Commons, owned my friend Beth. On the Uber ride, '90s rock band Third Eye Blind's "Jumper" was playing on the radio. Hearing the song almost felt like a sign, an ironic sign. The song is about a gay teenager who died by suicide after being bullied. I couldn't stay in my role and remain silent or leave the role and remain silent. I would no longer let myself be silent for marginalized voices.

When I arrived at the restaurant, my parents were waiting for me. I sat down with them at the mid-century modern, '70s-style table, both exasperated and relieved about the events leading up to that moment. While conversing with my parents and Beth, patrons of the restaurant were checking their phones, seeing my resignation pop up on their social media channels in real time, and then approaching our table to shake my hand.

My post very quickly received over a thousand likes and shares. I knew my resignation would make local headlines in Michigan and create a ripple in the craft beer industry, but I had no idea it would have such an effect on people and make national news. Within two hours of my resignation, the *Detroit Free Press* broke the story. Within twenty-four hours, NBC, *USA Today*, the *Chicago Tribune*, and just about every local and regional news outlet in between had covered my resignation. I was not expecting that!

It was uncomfortable. Fear of the unknown crept in. There was even more praise and criticism than when I took the position; everyone had an opinion, but this time, I didn't care. I learned to ignore the haters. I resigned without having another job, or even an inkling of another job. I resigned in order to use my voice as a platform, which would allow others who were silenced to finally have their voices heard. Within days of my resignation, the lawsuit settled in favor of the former employee.

I was a thirty-four-year-old, single, Black female executive in corporate America. I had worked so hard to climb that corporate ladder to get to where I was. I had broken the glass ceiling, for my age and demographics, in the beer industry, and in one life-changing decision, I risked it all and left it for the sake of integrity. It was terrifying, but I knew the importance of owning my truth and the importance of being present even when it's hard, even when it's scary. The time leading up to my resignation was the hardest, most tumultuous, awful time of my life. I didn't know what the outcome would be. In the words of Brené Brown, "I choose courage over comfort. I choose to be brave."

---

SOMETIMES WE DON'T KNOW how brave we can be until it is time to step up. We will face critics, but that cannot deter us. "It is not the critic who counts; the man who points out how the strong man stumbles, or where the doer of deeds could have done them better. The credit belongs to the man who is actually in the arena." Think about a time you were in the arena, when you knew you had to stand up for something you believed in. Think of that time you were faced with hard, tough decisions. What gave you the strength to keep standing in the arena? If you previously walked away from the arena, would you choose something differently next time?

**FIVE THINGS YOU CAN DO TO COMBAT DISCRIMINATION**

1   If you see something, say something. If you see an injustice happening around you, don't turn away and pretend you didn't see it. Sometimes, all it takes is one person to stand up to create change.

2   Report discrimination, racism, harassment, or other unjust acts if you witness them happening. Escalate an issue or situation to a teacher, professor, supervisor, HR, or someone in authority, such as security or law enforcement.

3   Be a support and/or offer a listening ear to the one being discriminated against. Listen to their experiences. When someone shares their experiences of discrimination, harassment, or bias with you, believe them.

4   Be a voice to those who have been marginalized. Your voice is powerful. If you have the privilege to speak up on behalf of someone else, help empower their voice and experiences, so they get the justice and validation they deserve.

5   Ensure policies and practices within an environment are equitable.

# 11

# Rising in Purpose

"'For I know the plans I have for you,' declares the Lord, 'plans to prosper you and not to harm you, plans to give you hope and a future.'"

**JEREMIAH 29:11**

FOR MUCH of my life, I looked for acceptance and belonging in others instead of focusing on my purpose and realizing the power to rise was already within me.

After my resignation, everyone asked, "What are you going to do next?"

My response was, "I don't know, but I know it's going to be something great, something that aligns with my integrity and ethics. I want to do something that will help create an impact."

So often we let our fears stunt us, and we miss out on opportunities that could enrich our lives. Quitting my job, without having another one, while others depended on me financially was a scary situation. It was a great risk. Most of us are fearful of the unknown and fearful of not knowing the outcome. We are often uncomfortable with the unfamiliar. It's scary, but we need to get into the habit of getting comfortable with being uncomfortable. Growth comes from discomfort—not just growth for us, but also growth for others. I learned to have faith in my future instead of fear over my circumstance.

A couple of weeks after my resignation, while praying and meditating on a flight back to Grand Rapids from a long-weekend getaway in Los Angeles, an inkling and burning passion to start my own company popped into my mind. In my head, I was naming a list of companies I'd like to work for. I knew I wanted to work for an organization that was committed to doing the work of diversity, equity, and inclusion. It dawned on me: *Why can't I create that company?* Why not start my own business and have control of which companies I work with? I had never had a desire to be an entrepreneur, and quite frankly as a single Black millennial female, I never even thought it was possible. Representation is powerful. We are drawn to achieve and be what we can see. I had not previously personally known someone with a similar identity who was doing something comparable, but if I had, I'm sure the thought of it wouldn't have sounded so foreign to me.

I had a peace from God that starting my own business was what I was supposed to be doing—so I followed that. On November 15, 2019, I started Graci LLC, my diversity, equity, and inclusion consulting, training, and public-speaking business. I partner with organizations that are committed to building more inclusive environments where members work more authentically.

As a result of my resignation making national headlines, new headlines emerged locally and within the beer industry as I announced the creation of my business on social media. Within a short time, business was booming. By the end of December 2019, my 2020 calendar was booked full of client consulting gigs and speaking engagements. I was ready for a business journey of the unknown. On March 4, 2020, I was the keynote speaker for nearly a thousand people, and then the next week the whole world shut down due to a global pandemic.

All my clients stated they no longer had diversity budget, and every conference and seminar I was scheduled to speak at was canceled. By the end of March 2020, the rest of my calendar year of work was canceled. Without an income, and having all of the time in the world, I decided to invest in writing this memoir full-time. I remained grounded in my faith and persevered in doing DEI work, even if I didn't have an audience at the time. I knew the COVID-19 global pandemic couldn't last forever, and the work of diversity, equity, and inclusion would be important work our society would continue to need.

ON MAY 25, 2020, MUCH OF THE WORLD was rocked by witnessing the murder of George Floyd by the hands, or knee rather, of a police officer. For some of us, it was brand new—something we had never experienced before—for others it was another name, another Black man wrongfully killed at the hands of law enforcement. We had experienced or witnessed injustices like this for our entire lives. Some folks didn't understand why people were rioting and what the big deal was. Some even sided with the police officer, believing the murder was warranted, saying, "He shouldn't have resisted." "If he would have just…"

All of my clients who stated they didn't have diversity budget and didn't prioritize the work of diversity, equity, and inclusion suddenly were in desperate need for DEI and unconscious bias training "yesterday," and just like that, I was back to work. We didn't get to this place of injustice and inequity in society because of George Floyd or Derek Chauvin. We have been in this place for our entire lives, for lifetimes, because of

We have been in this place
for our entire lives, for lifetimes,
because of the continuous injustices
and inequitable practices institutionally,
generationally, and systemically.

the continuous injustices and inequitable practices institutionally, generationally, and systemically. We are in this place because we haven't continually valued people for the identities they are, backgrounds they have, and journeys they've lived.

After George Floyd's murder, our society entered into the largest modern-day civil rights movement we have experienced since the 1960s. Many across the United States and across the world joined together in solidarity, marching in protests. During those protests, I felt like the Black and Brown brothers, sisters, and siblings I was marching with were family. Solidarity connects us: longing for, striving for, marching for, standing for the same thing—equality and justice.

Everyone responds to trauma differently. During that time, I often wept with my close friends. Weeping in anger and weeping in sadness for the loss of George Floyd and many others like him: Emmett Till, Rodney King, Trayvon Martin, Eric Garner, Michael Brown . . . and so many countless others. It could have been me. Close White friends of mine—Amy, Jonathan, Beth, Dave, and Chasity—all reached out to me with arms open wide saying, "We may never understand, because we have never had to live that fear because of the color of our skin, but we are with you, stand with you, and will protest with you."

They are great examples of what it means to be an ally. To show up for someone, to march or protest with them, to use your voice for them, to listen to them, even when you've never shared the same trauma or experience.

Some were responding to trauma by rioting. There was an uproar of why people were rioting. Some were rioting because they had been silenced for their whole lives and had an opportunity to lash out, to be heard, or at least to be noticed. Some were rioting as a form of expression after months of not having their typical outlets due to the global pandemic. Some were rioting to create destruction, separate from justice. Violence is never the solution; it only contributes to the problem.

When we are more upset about damage to our buildings than we are about the wrongful deaths of innocent Black and Brown people, we are contributing to the problem, not the solution. We are so quick in repairing physical damages from violence; when we pick up a hammer, we also need to hold a hammer of accountability within our law enforcement system. When we put dollars behind corporations, we need to hold those corporations accountable to their actions and demand equitable practices. When we board up windows, we also need to board up our racial biases. When we read instructions, we also need to ask questions and be open when we don't understand. When we look both ways before crossing the street, we need to look all ways—into the journeys of others. When we rush to the streets, we also need to rush to the ballots to vote for equitable leaders. When we break down our toolbox, we need to break down systemic and institutional barriers.

At the time of writing, it is 2022, and I am thirty-seven years old. The demand for diversity, equity, and inclusion work is higher than it's ever been. Since I began in this field, organizations have also started prioritizing belonging, accessibility, and justice in their work. My work with clients as a DEI consultant, trainer, and speaker now spans clients across the globe. To each client, I tell my story, why this work is personal to me, and how together we can work toward a more inclusive and equitable world.

Since I started writing this memoir, we have experienced so many unjust deaths, I mean murders, of Ahmaud Arbery—a runner, shot "running while Black" in a White neighborhood; Breonna Taylor—an emergency medical technician, shot by police in a "no-knock warrant" in the hunt for someone else;

Patrick Lyoya—an immigrant from the Democratic Republic of the Congo, shot by police, execution-style, after resisting arrest on a Monday morning traffic stop only five miles from my house. In recent years, we have experienced a drastic increase of hate crimes against and murders of Black, Brown, Indigenous, and Asian communities. I know it can feel overwhelming, and that sometimes we feel helpless, but our fight for justice and equity must continue until all lives are treated as if they matter.

We can't be part of the solution until we work on the root cause and take responsibility for our own actions. When we are able to see ourselves as a part of a dimension of diversity, we are able to be a part of the solution of inclusion. The only way we're able to reduce hate and discrimination is when we finally start seeing and valuing one another for who we are. The work of diversity, equity, and inclusion never stops. The work is continuous and requires accountability—accountability to ourselves and to our peers. What actionable steps are you committed to taking in your life to embrace diversity, overcome bias, increase equity, and rise in inclusion?

———————

WE CAN THINK ABOUT HOW FAR we have to go, but we also must celebrate how far we've come and how far you've personally come on your journey. You are powerful. It all starts with one person. Nearly each morning, sun or snow, Teddy and I run two miles through the downtown streets of Grand Rapids. During the run, I meditate on how far *I've* come and create goals for the future, claiming these goals and speaking them into existence. I imagine what my biological mother's life has been like, giving me up, living through trauma and civil unrest, nearly dying of starvation, meeting me in 2015, and then her life now. I ponder about what my life would have been like if I hadn't been adopted and if I had survived in the Congo, in comparison to my life here in the United States, with a big, loving family, siblings and siblings-in-law, ten nieces and nephews, a great niece, a great nephew, and my mom and dad living part-time in the Congo and part-time near Grand Rapids. I think about my close friends who are dear to my heart, celebrating together in the highs and leaning on each other during the lows of our journeys. We have all come so far.

In a video chat conversation with MariJani, Musa, Mom, and Dad in the Congo recently, MariJani, reflecting on her journey, exclaimed, "If you didn't give me food and care, I would die. I am happy and I rejoice." She gave me up to save my life. Thirty years later, I returned to the Congo to help save her life. Both of our journeys of survival and rising started with just one person.

All it takes is one person—one person to believe, one person to stand, one person to support, one person to speak, one person to act—and the rest can be supported by a village.

Life is a journey. You don't have to be born in a mud hut to have a story. We all have a story, and we *all* have a purpose. We all go through the adversities, the obstacles, and the challenges which get us down and try to hold us back. By the grace of God, I was found and God knew my story wasn't going to end there: my story isn't just for me, it's for all of us to know we aren't alone. I know the journey isn't easy—there will continue to be risks, sideways turns, and tormenting situations. Through the challenges, our paths may look much different from what we had originally planned, but our purpose is worth living, even through the obstacles, challenges, and adversities. When we are our authentic selves, living our purpose, our power is limitless.

## HOW TO BE AN ALLY

1   Be present. Speak directly. Make eye contact. Have body language that shows you're open to listening.

2   Show support. Voice and communicate support in an actionable way.

3   Listen and seek to understand. Listen to hear, don't listen to respond.

4   Meet people where they are. Don't have expectations for them to be in a mental or emotional place they aren't in.

5   Use your privilege as a platform, a voice, and as empowerment for others.

6   Use your platforms and voice for others with less access or privilege.

7   Check in on the mental health and well-being of others.

8   Actively listen to stories about bias or mistreatment.

9   If you see something, say something to confront it. Don't be afraid to speak up. Your voice can really matter, even if it makes an impact on one person.

10   Acknowledge or give credit to others for their ideas and work.

11   Take a public stand to support equality. It's easy to silently support others, but nobody knows we are doing it. Publicly advocate for equality and equity. This means even more.

12   Mentor or sponsor someone with less privilege. Your access, knowledge, and skill can help advance and empower others more than you realize.

You don't have to be
born in a mud hut to have a
story. We all have a story, and
we *all* have a purpose.

---

MY MISSION THOUGH MY WORK and through this book is to help empower you to use your voice, speak your truth, embrace your identities, value others, and bring your whole self to this world—so you can live and work more authentically. Our power comes through our voices and our actions—individually and collectively. I may not know you personally, but I see you. I value you. I am with you. *Through our journeys and through every adversity, we all have the power to rise.*

# Acknowledgments

T O CHARLSIE DEWEY: You were the first one who encouraged me to write a book and share my story. You were also
the first one who covered my story in the media when I
discovered MariJani was alive. You helped give me the strength
and courage to keep telling my story. Thank you for being
an amazing journalist, news director, and incredible friend.

To Richelle Fredson: Thank you for believing in the power of
my story. I'm so grateful to have had you early in the process as
my book coach! Thank you for teaching me how to be an author
and connect with my readers. I'm forever grateful for you going
above and beyond your job description by continuously press-
ing the best agents and publishers to read my book proposal.
Your work and advocacy landed me the greatest book deal.

To Page Two and Macmillan Publishers: Page Two co-owner
Jesse Finkelstein, from our very first interaction, I knew you
were the publisher for me! Everything in my soul aligned with
your work. Thank you for believing in my story and enabling it
to be shared with the world. To my editor, Emily Schultz—you
are what I prayed for. Thank you for helping me dive deeper,

even when I didn't want to. Your vision is everything my story needed. I'm quite certain you now know me better than anyone. Thank you for guiding me in this journey. Thank you to Jen Lum and the design team; your work is incredible. To the Page Two marketing team and Macmillan sales and distribution teams, it was once a pipe dream to see my book on a shelf; thank you for loving my story and selling it everywhere books are sold. You've made my pipe dream become a reality. To my project manager, Adrineh Der-Boghossian, and everyone behind the scenes who has worked on my book, thank you. I appreciate you!

To Arena Place: Ater Grondman, Dayle Braden, Emily Krygier, and Peri McCracken, you've supported Teddy and me during my book journey for the last three years. Thank you for being my cheerleaders, nearly every day of the week, and helping me keep my eye on the prize.

To Brian Kelly: I've greatly admired your work since the day I met you at the receptionist desk at Varnum. After I asked for you autograph, which I still have by the way, one of my goals was to one day buy a piece of your work. Having you as my photographer for my book jacket is a dream come true. Thank you for your talent in bringing my vision to life.

To Misael DeJesus: I'm so grateful we have been brought together! Your hair, makeup, personal assistant skills, talent, and creativity created magic for the jacket photos! "When it's right, it's right." You are the right person who I needed on this journey. Thank you for bringing me ease and comfort, from the most tense to the most fun situations.

To Beth Rich: Thank you for your friendship and support during this entire book journey. So many moments of joy were spent celebrating together at The Commons, while moments of sadness or frustration were also spent together. Through it all, you've been there.

To TEKsystems: The leaders who equipped me to reach my potential and the colleagues I worked alongside, who relentlessly supported me, are the epitome of an inclusive work environment. To Alex Pulido, Christie Paakkonen, Jon Carpenter, and Craig Kapuscinski, you always saw more potential in me than I saw in myself. Thank you for pushing me to be greater in my roles. You've shaped me to be who I am. To TEK West Michigan and TEK Inclusion & Diversity team, I am forever impacted by you. TEK West Michigan continues to feel like home. TEK Inclusion & Diversity team, your investment in me was the catalyst to me living my purpose. You gave me the platform of my first stage. Thank you for equipping me to work in my passion. Franklin Reed and Ian Moses, you taught me how to connect with my audience and be a public speaker. To Craig Kapuscinski, Kristen VanDenBerge, and Janey Fry, you are always with me. The triangle never dies.

To you: Thank you for reading my book! Thank you for taking the time to read, reflect, and share with others. You make me want to pinch myself. Your support means the world!

To those who are allies: Thank you. We need your voices now more than ever before. Allies are the ones who helped empower me to be the person I am today. Your impact is greater than you may ever realize.

To my siblings: I'm so grateful to be a part of our family. Throughout my life, I've admired you all and have strived to embody many traits and accomplishments you've all obtained and achieved. From cars, to culture, to work ethic, you continue to influence and inspire me.

To Ted and Jennifer Harkema: I still cherish talking to you on the phone. After my resignation, I felt like my world was falling apart, and you told me you were proud of me. Thank you for being there for me.

To my biological mother, MariJani: You are the bravest, most courageous person I know. Meeting you for the first time will forever be the happiest day of my life. Thank you for giving me life. I strive to make you proud and live a legacy of your wildest dreams.

To my mom and dad, Jayn and Ray Harkema: You're the two most amazing people I've ever met. You truly embody God's love. Thank you for giving me the opportunity of life and choosing me to be your daughter! I am so proud to be your daughter. Thank you for encouraging me to pursue every dream and aspiration, including writing this book. I'm so grateful for your unconditional love.

To God: I spent so many years praying so many prayers wishing I was someone else, anyone else. I now understand why you created me to be the person I am. My experiences need to be lived and shared, not just for myself but for others. Thank you for helping me strive to be a vessel of your grace. Without you, I am nothing.

# Notes

p. 23   *A microaggression or micro-behavior is . . .* Dictionary.com, s.v. "microaggression," dictionary.com/browse/microaggression.

p. 27   *Bias is "a prejudice in favor of or against . . .* "Glossary of Bias Terms," Washington University in St. Louis, students.wustl.edu/glossary-bias-terms/.

p. 28   *Legal scholar and author Kenji Yoshino defines covering as . . .* Kenji Yoshino, *Covering: The Hidden Assault on Our Civil Rights* (Random House, 2006).

p. 81   *"Suicide is a leading cause of death in the United States . . .* "Facts about Suicide," Centers for Disease Control and Prevention, cdc.gov/suicide/facts/index.html.

p. 81   *people who identify as sexual minorities have higher rates of suicide attempts . . .* "Disparities in Suicide," Centers for Disease Control and Prevention, cdc.gov/suicide/facts/disparities-in-suicide.html.

p. 81   *the following are signs someone may be contemplating suicide . . .* "Risk of Suicide," National Alliance on Mental Illness, nami.org/About-Mental-Illness/Common-with-Mental-Illness/Risk-of-Suicide.

p. 98   *"Team performance improves by 50% when everyone feels included." . . .* "Inclusion Starts with I," Accenture, June 23, 2017, youtube.com/watch?v=2g88Ju6nkcg&t=2s.

p. 101   *"People are hard to hate close up. Move in." . . .* Brené Brown, *Braving the Wilderness: The Quest for True Belonging and the Courage to Stand Alone* (Random House, 2017).

p. 106   *According to a 2021 study by McKinsey & Company and Lean In* ... *Women in the Workplace 2021*, McKinsey & Company and Lean In, wiw-report.s3.amazonaws.com/Women_in_the _Workplace_2021.pdf.

p. 109   *More than one in every four adults* ... "Mental Health Disorder Statistics," Johns Hopkins Medicine, hopkinsmedicine.org /health/wellness-and-prevention/mental-health-disorder -statistics.

p. 116   *The Kübler-Ross Grief Cycle brings us through the five stages of grief.* .. "The Five Stages of Grief," Psycom, June 7, 2022, psycom.net/stages-of-grief.

p. 169   *Former Facebook COO Sheryl Sandberg states* ... "Careers Aren't Ladders, They're Jungle Gyms," Stanford GSB's *View from the Top*, November 30, 2018, gsb.stanford.edu/insights/shery -sandberg-careers-arent-ladders-theyre-jungle-gyms.

p. 173   *It is not the critic who counts* ... quoted in Erin McCarthy, "Roosevelt's 'The Man in the Arena,'" *Mental Floss*, April 23, 2015, mentalfloss.com/article/63389/roosevelts-man-arena.

p. 180   *"Only when we are brave enough to explore the darkness* ... Brené Brown, *The Gifts of Imperfection: Let Go of Who You Think You're Supposed to Be and Embrace Who You Are* (Hazelden Publishing, 2010).

p. 184   *"I choose courage over comfort* ... Brené Brown, *Brené Brown: The Call to Courage*, dir. Sandra Restrepo (Netflix, 2019).

# About the Author

GRACI HARKEMA is the owner of Graci LLC, an international consultancy providing training and speaking on diversity, equity, inclusion, and unconscious bias for Fortune 500 companies, small businesses, and non-profit organizations. *Grand Rapids Business Journal* named Graci a 40 Under 40 Business Leader in West Michigan, one of the 50 Most Influential Women in West Michigan, and one of the 200 Most Powerful Business Leaders in West Michigan. Graci received national media attention in 2019 for publicly resigning from a prominent diversity and inclusion leadership role to make a stand for racial equity and justice. Passionate about serving her community, she volunteers on LGBTQ+ non-profit boards. She is also an avid supporter of her parents' faith-based non-profit, Heart for Central Africa, in her hometown of Bukavu, Democratic Republic of the Congo. A graduate in communications from Grand Valley State University, Graci resides in Grand Rapids, Michigan, with her dog, Teddy Roosevelt.

# Let's Rise Together

Dictionary.com defines *rise* as: "To come into existence. To come into action. To move from a lower to a higher position; move upward. To advance to a higher level of action, thought, feeling, act."

After reading *Rising*, I hope you feel inspired, empowered, and seen. Are you ready to rise?

If you were inspired by my book, bring me to your organization. I'm available for leadership and team training workshops and keynote addresses. I'd love to help inspire those who are in your life.

If you were empowered by my book, let's be friends. Follow me and feel free to slide into my DMs to tell me what you thought of the book. Follow me on Instagram: **@thegraciharkema**. If Instagram isn't your thing, follow my business page on Facebook: **Graci LLC**. If Instagram and Facebook aren't your things, follow me on Twitter: **@GraciHarkema.**

Were there parts of my book that resonated with you or moved you? I would love to hear about it. Share it on social media and tag me. Share it socially, on online author forums, or IRL with a loved one, colleague, friend, or family member. Your voice is powerful.

If you were inspired or empowered by my book, give it a rating. Reviews do matter. I would really love it if you wrote me a review on your preferred retailer's website.

If you want more from me, visit **graciharkema.com** and get exclusive content by signing up for my newsletter.

If you'd like to get in contact with me directly, visit **graciharkema .com/contact** or send me a direct message on social media.

Thank you! I look forward to rising together!

Life is a journey. Even in the most challenging moments, remember that you aren't alone and that you have the power to rise.